TOP-RATED
GROUND
COVERS
AND HOW TO USE THEM IN YOUR GARDEN

This book was produced for Western Publishing Company, Inc., by the staff of Horticultural Associates, Inc.

Executive Producer: Richard M. Ray
Contributing Authors: Alvin Horton, Robert L. Stebbins, Lance Walheim
Consultants: John Ford, Ralph Miller, Robert Ticknor
Photography: Michael Landis
Art Director: Richard Baker
Book Design and Production: Lingke Moeis
Associate Editor: Lance Walheim
Research Editor: Randy Peterson
Copy Editors: Greg Boucher, Miriam Boucher
Production Editor: Kathleen Parker
Illustrations: Charles Hoeppner, Roy Jones
Typography: Linda Encinas
Additional Photography: William Aplin, Pamela Harper, Victor Reiter, Susan A. Roth
Cover Photo: Michael Landis
Acknowledgements: Chalet Bernensis Inn, St. Helena, CA; Richard Pernice, Napa, CA; William Robinson, Japanese Garden Society of Oregon; Eleanor Sprando, Portland, OR; Steve's Hardware, St. Helena, CA; Whiting's Nursery, St. Helena, CA; Stacy Wong, Portland, OR.

For Golden Press:

Publisher: Jonathan P. Latimer
Senior Editor: Susan A. Roth
Associate Editor: Karen Stray Nolting

 Golden Press • New York

Western Publishing Company, Inc.

Racine, Wisconsin

Top-Rated Ground Covers

The plants we call ground covers are a diverse group linked more by a similar use in the landscape than by any similarity in appearance. A ground cover is thought of as any low-growing plant that, when planted en masse, grows thickly enough to blanket the ground.

Vines deprived of anything to climb upon function as ground covers; varieties of evergreen or deciduous shrubs with prostrate or spreading limbs, such as junipers or cotoneasters, can be planted as ground covers; evergreen and deciduous herbaceous perennials with creeping stems or roots are very popular ground covers.

In the landscape: Lawn grass is still the most widely grown ground cover. However, other plants can enliven a landscape with interesting textures and foliage patterns, colorful flowers or berries, and create a visual excitement that no lawn can.

Practicality combines with beauty when ground covers are planted, because most can check or retard erosion, serve as a living mulch to retain soil moisture and discourage weeds, and provide visual carpeting. Specially suited ground covers blanket problem areas where rocks, exposed tree roots, dryness, wetness, shade, or heat discourage or prohibit other garden plants.

Top-rated: The plants discussed in this book were chosen as being the best ground covers for North American gardens. They are considered *top-rated* because they were selected by expert gardeners and horticulturists as being reliable plants that are easy to grow and readily available.

At left: Ground covers add rich texture and visual interest to the landscape, while solving problems on difficult sites.

Burford holly (*Ilex cornuta*)

Aaron's beard (*Hypericum calycinum*)

Garden verbena (*Verbena peruviana*)

Hall's Japanese honeysuckle (*Lonicera japonica* 'Halliana')

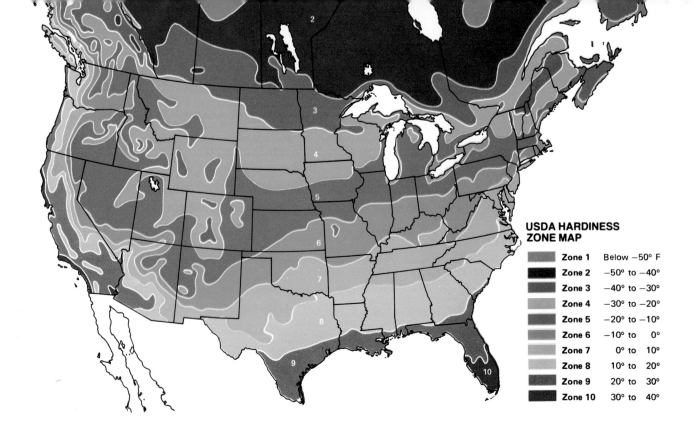

USDA HARDINESS ZONE MAP

	Zone 1	Below −50° F
	Zone 2	−50° to −40°
	Zone 3	−40° to −30°
	Zone 4	−30° to −20°
	Zone 5	−20° to −10°
	Zone 6	−10° to 0°
	Zone 7	0° to 10°
	Zone 8	10° to 20°
	Zone 9	20° to 30°
	Zone 10	30° to 40°

Climates For Ground Covers

Climate determines which plants will grow where you live. A ground cover's adaptability to a location, as with any other kind of plant, depends upon precipitation, temperature, humidity, soil, weather patterns, and length of seasons. Temperature extremes—both winter cold and summer heat—are probably the most important factors in influencing a garden plant's suitability for your climate.

Hardiness zones: The USDA plant hardiness map, above, divides the US and Canada into 10 zones according to winter temperatures; the average minimum temperature of each zone differs from that of adjacent zones by 10 degrees Fahrenheit.

Each plant entry lists the range of zones where the plant is recommended. This indicates the plant's tolerance to both cold and warm climates. For example, woolly yarrow *(Achillea tomentosa)* adapts to temperatures in Zones 3 to 9. The following chart and the encyclopedia section of this book use the USDA zone numbers where each ground cover will give a top-rated performance.·

Climate regions: Since a plant's adaptation to a climate is influenced by other factors than temperature, the climate region map is useful as an additional aid to selecting ground covers adaptable to your region. The continent is divided into 10 climate regions on the basis of a combination of climatic factors. These include humidity, wind, temperature fluctuation and extremes, predominant soil type, duration of the growing season, and patterns of precipitation.

Climate regions where each of the top-rated ground cover plants are adapted are indicated in the chart on the following pages. After you locate your climate region, the chart will tell you at a glance which ground covers adapt dependably to your climate. Keep in mind, of course, that boundaries between regions on this map and between zones in the USDA map are approximate because of variability and unpredictability of climate.

Coordinating hardiness zones and regions of adaptation: As a rule, for a ground cover to be suited to your area, it must be recommended for both your hardiness zone and your climate region. As you study the chart and the maps, you will notice that USDA Zones 8 to 10 are particularly complex in the western United States. Frequent irrigation is necessary in that dry-summer area unless drought-tolerant plants are selected. Even with irrigation, some humidity-loving plants do not adapt well. Conversely, native Western plants such as certain species of *Ceanothus* (California lilac) and *Baccharis* (dwarf coyote brush) thrive in the West but often languish or die in the same USDA zones elsewhere because summer rain and high humidity combined with high temperatures harm them. Therefore, the regional adaptation map and the chart on the following pages are helpful—and sometimes essential—supplements to USDA temperature zones when it comes to choosing the best plants for your climate.

4

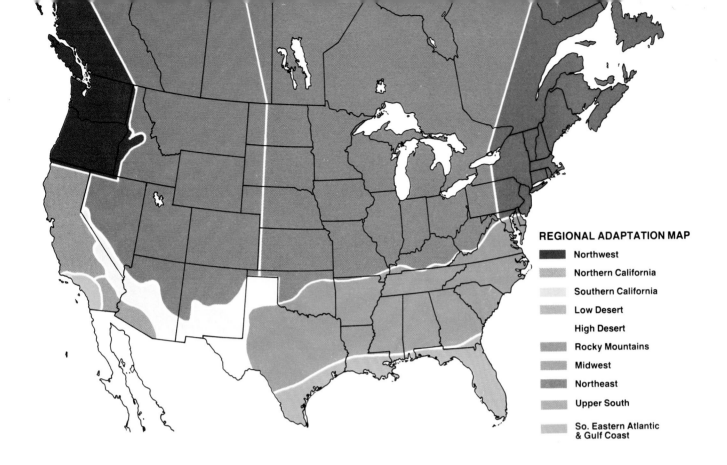

REGIONAL ADAPTATION MAP

- Northwest
- Northern California
- Southern California
- Low Desert
- High Desert
- Rocky Mountains
- Midwest
- Northeast
- Upper South
- So. Eastern Atlantic & Gulf Coast

Microclimates: Each region of the country has a predictable general climate—average amounts of rainfall and snowfall, average high and low temperatures, and average frost dates. But within each region, there are variations in that general climate due to such influences as elevation and the proximity to large bodies of water and to cities. Within a USDA climate zone there are always some spots where the average minimum temperature is significantly lower or higher than the general average minimum temperature. There are large and tiny islands of Zones 3 and 5 within Zone 4, for example, which are created by extreme changes in elevation or the moderating influence of lakes.

Because of one or a combination of several very localized climatic conditions such as high winds or scant rainfall, a climate region may contain areas where ground covers not recommended for that region will flourish—or where some recommended for that region will not. For instance, in a Zone 7 lakeside spot where winter climate is moderated by the lake, a ground cover whose lowest climate zone is Zone 8, or even Zone 9, may thrive. In the "rain shadow" of a hill in the Midwest, relative dryness might necessitate irrigation to grow a ground cover that requires none in most of the Midwest.

Within your own property, there are slight variations in temperatures, intensity of sunlight, and exposure to wind, due to the effects of sloping land and to the position of your house, tall trees, and fences. Sun reflecting off a south-facing wall warms the nearby area. A low spot at the bottom of a hill collects cold air and is the first place to experience frost. The northern side of your property, which is probably shaded most of the day by your house, is generally colder than the rest of your property. Elsewhere in your garden, a sheltering, heat-retaining wall or rock outcrop can create another warm microclimate. These areas, with tiny localized climate personalities all their own, are called *microclimates*.

During frosty weather, slopes may be relatively, or entirely, frost-free, but in areas where cold air is trapped from flowing downhill by walls, fences, or hedges, there will be frost, perhaps heavy frost. Ground covers insulated by snow in most of your landscape may be too tender for a corner of the house where cold wind blasts away insulating layers of snow and exposes the plants to desiccating winter sun. Such microclimates can both extend and limit your choice of ground covers.

Ground covers themselves can create comfortable microclimates. For example, they make a house cooler than it would be if it were surrounded by bare earth or paving.

If you learn to recognize the warm and cold microclimates in your yard, you'll be able to choose the best ground covers for your planting sites. Plants that are borderline hardy for your area may do well if you take protective measures such as providing wind or snow shelters and making use of your property's warm microclimates. With protection, plants can often be grown successfully in the next colder zone.

5

In most climates, bugleweed (*Ajuga reptans*) forms a dense mat brightened by spikes of flowers in spring and early summer.

In warm climates, cape weed (*Arctotheca calendula*) quickly creates a drought-tolerant cover on well-drained, sunny sites.

Regional Adaptation

Name	Zones	Northwest, W. Canada	Northern California	Southern California	Low Desert	High Desert	Rocky Mountains	Midwest, Central Canada	Northeast, E. Canada	Upper South	Southeastern Atlantic, Gulf Coast
Abelia grandiflora 'Prostrata'	6-10	■	■	■	■	■		■	■	■	■
Achillea tomentosa	3-9	■	■	■	■	■	■	■	■	■	■
Aegopodium podagraria	3-9	■	■			■	■	■	■		
Aizoaceae sp.	8-10*		■	■	■						
Ajuga reptans	4-10	■	■	■		■	■	■	■	■	■
Arctostaphylos uva-ursi	2-8	■	■	■			■	■	■	■	
Arctotheca calendula	9-10		■	■	■						
Arenaria verna	3-9*	■	■	■			■	■	■	■	
Baccharis pilularis	8-10		■	■	■	■					
Berberis thunbergii 'Crimson Pygmy'	4-9	■	■			■	■	■	■	■	
Bougainvillea sp.	9-10		■	■	■						■
Calluna vulgaris	4-7	■	■					■	■		
Campanula poscharskyana	3-8	■	■	■			■	■	■	■	
Carissa grandiflora	10			■	■						■
Ceanothus sp.	8-10	■	■	■							
Ceratostigma plumbaginoides	6-9	■	■	■				■	■	■	■
Chamaemelum nobile	5-10	■	■	■	■	■	■	■	■	■	■
Cistus sp.	8-10	■	■	■	■						
Convallaria majalis	3-9	■	■				■	■	■	■	
Convolvulus cneorum	7-10		■	■	■					■	■
Coprosma x kirkii	9-10		■	■							
Cotoneaster sp.	5-10	■	■	■	■	■	■	■	■	■	■
Cytisus x kewensis	6-9	■	■						■	■	
Duchesnea indica	5-10	■	■	■	■	■	■	■	■	■	■

Regional Adaptation

Name	Zones	Northwest, W. Canada	Northern California	Southern California	Low Desert	High Desert	Rocky Mountains	Midwest, Central Canada	Northeast, E. Canada	Upper South	Southeastern Atlantic, Gulf Coast
Erica carnea	4-8	■	■	■				■	■	■	
Euonymus fortunei radicans	4-8	■	■	■	■	■		■	■		
Festuca ovina glauca	5-10	■	■	■	■	■	■	■	■	■	
Fragaria chiloensis	4-8	■	■	■	■	■	■	■	■	■	■
Galium odoratum	4-10	■	■				■	■	■	■	■
Gardenia jasminoides 'Radicans'	8-10		■	■	■					■	■
Gaultheria procumbens	4-8	■	■					■		■	
Gazania sp.	9-10		■	■	■						
Genista lydia	6-9	■	■							■	
Hedera helix	5-10	■	■	■	■	■	■	■	■	■	■
Hemerocallis hybrids	2-10*	■	■	■	■	■	■	■	■	■	■
Herniaria glabra	6-10	■	■	■	■	■					
Hosta sp.	3-9	■	■	■	■		■	■	■	■	■
Hypericum calycinum	5-10	■	■	■	■	■	■	■	■	■	■
Iberis sempervirens	3-10	■	■	■			■	■	■	■	■
Ilex sp.	6-10*	■	■	■			■	■	■	■	■
Juniperus sp.	2-10*	■	■	■	■	■	■	■	■	■	■
Lantana montevidensis	9-10		■	■	■					■	■
Laurentia fluviatilis	9-10		■	■							■
Liriope sp.	5-10*		■	■				■	■	■	■
Lonicera japonica 'Halliana'	4-10	■	■	■	■	■	■	■	■	■	■
Mahonia repens	4-10	■	■	■	■	■	■	■	■	■	■
Myoporum parvifolium	9-10	■	■	■							
Nandina domestica 'Harbour Dwarf'	6-10	■	■	■	■	■	■			■	■
Ophiopogon sp.	5-10		■	■	■			■	■	■	■
Osteospermum fruticosum	8-10	■	■	■							
Pachysandra terminalis	4-9	■	■	■			■	■	■	■	■
Paxistima sp.	5-9	■	■		■		■	■	■	■	
Pittosporum tobira 'Wheeler's Dwarf'	8-10	■	■	■		■				■	■
Polygonum sp.	4-10*	■	■	■	■	■	■	■	■	■	■
Potentilla tabernaemontani	4-10	■	■	■	■	■	■	■	■	■	■
Pyracantha sp.	6-10	■	■	■	■		■	■	■	■	■
Rosmarinus officinalis 'Lockwood de Forest'	7-10	■	■	■	■	■			■	■	■
Sagina subulata (See *Arenaria verna*.)											
Sarcococca hookerana humilis	7-10	■	■	■						■	■
Sedum sp.	3-10*	■	■	■	■	■	■	■	■	■	■
Soleirolia soleirolii	8-10	■	■	■						■	■
Taxus baccata 'Repandens'	6-9	■	■	■			■	■	■	■	
Thymus sp.	3-10	■	■	■	■	■	■	■	■	■	■
Trachelospermum jasminoides	8-10		■	■	■	■				■	■
Verbena peruviana	8-10		■	■	■	■					
Vinca major	8-10		■	■	■						■
Vinca minor	5-10	■	■	■	■	■	■	■	■	■	■
Waldsteinia fragarioides	4-9	■	■	■				■	■	■	■

*Variable among species. See encyclopedia text.

Using Ground Covers in Your Garden

Ground covers make up a unique group of landscape plants—they are the only permanent plants that can provide a sweep of greenery or color without blocking your view or creating a closed-in feeling. Unlike a lawn, they act as a physical barrier, but like a lawn, they do not create a visual barrier.

As with most landscape plants, ground covers serve a dual purpose. They are planted both for the beauty of their foliage or flowers and also to serve many practical functions. There are many ways you can use these dependable and attractive plants to improve the appearance and value of your property.

BEAUTIFYING WITH GROUND COVERS

Professional landscapers know how important ground covers are to giving a garden a finished look. Ground covers can create a sense of completeness by blending trees, shrubs, and house into a unified setting. The most effective ways you can provide that finishing touch are described below.

Border: A bed of ground cover planted along the edge of a walk, path, or driveway creates a softening border that blends the feature into the natural landscape. The plants also lead your eye along the path. Pachysandra, English ivy, and junipers are widely used for this purpose.

Carpet: While a grass lawn is nearly everyone's ideal outdoor carpet because of its fine texture and ability to

At left: Juniper (*Juniperus* sp.) creates a year-round carpet of green on sloped ground.

Wild strawberry (*Fragaria chiloensis*)

Bush ice plant (*Aizoaceae*)

Periwinkle (*Vinca minor*)

African daisy (*Gazania* sp.)

Scotch moss (*Arenaria verna* 'Aurea') makes an elegant mat of foliage and tolerates light foot traffic.

Creeping thyme (*Thymus praecox arcticus*) spreads by underground runners and fills in beautifully between stepping stones.

A steep slope can be dramatically landscaped with rocks and low, spreading shrubs such as juniper (*Juniperus* sp.).

withstand foot traffic, it demands constant care to keep it looking good. And every square foot of the landscape planted in lawn must be smooth enough for, and accessible to, a mower.

Numerous ground covers, on the other hand, require little care and carpet uneven and hard-to-maintain spots beautifully. Few, however, accept much foot traffic. (See the list of ground covers that tolerate light foot traffic on page 16.) If you want to carpet areas that will have no (or very occasional) foot traffic, your ground cover choices are vast. (See page 15.) Use a carpet of green or colorful ground cover to replace part of a large lawn, on slopes, or in other areas where lawns grow poorly and are difficult to maintain.

Break up expanse: Though a large expanse of lawn provides a pleasing open feeling, it can be boring to look at and a nuisance to mow. A more friendly, but still open, look can be created by bordering and breaking up the monotonous expanse of lawn with large sweeps of low to medium-height ground cover plants. These create a carpet of a different color and texture that contrasts beautifully with the carpet of lawn.

Between paving stones: Certain ground covers are right at home growing in the niches between flagstones and bricks. Kinds that tolerate light foot traffic dress up the stepping stones in a path through a flower bed or herb garden and turn a flagstone patio into a cool retreat.

Unify a setting: Ground covers are unexcelled for unifying the landscape. Planting ground covers around and beneath various landscape elements creates harmony by tying them together visually and softening harsh lines and stark or rough surfaces.

For instance, when several trees are strung out randomly across a lawn, they can be turned into a landscape asset if they are underplanted with an expanse of ground cover that extends beyond the outer limbs of the trees. The ground cover links the trees that would otherwise vie with each other for attention into a unified feature.

Architectural features are more at home in the natural setting when combined with plants. Serbian bellflower can fill chinks and seams in stone stairs with softening leaves and flowers. Japanese spurge makes a strong transitional link between a tree-backed shrub planting and a patio or driveway.

Low barrier: Many ground covers —particularly ones with needled foliage or sharp thorns, or that grow to knee-height—discourage both people and pets from walking on them. Planted on the edges of your property, or wherever you do not want people to tread, these ground covers create a natural barrier but do not block light or vision.

For accents: Some ground covers, such as hostas, African daisies, or daylilies, when used in large clumps or small drifts can accent nearby landscape features. Planted beside birdbaths, statuary, lampposts, benches, decorative gateways, or other garden ornaments, they draw your eye because of their bold textures or colors.

Companions: Ground covers are often planted as companions for shrubs, bulbs, or perennials. Evergreen ground covers dress the bare ground in shrubbery borders or bulb beds year round. For shrubs that do their best in cool, moist soil, ground covers beneath their branches will provide a living mulch that keeps soil cool.

Select companions whose textures and colors create interesting visual combinations and whose cultural needs are similar. Root systems of many—but not all— ground covers are shallow and unaggressive and will not compete with those of their companions.

Low, drought-tolerant covers such as chamomile and creeping thyme make perfect companions for crocus or other small bulbs, harmonizing with them as they bloom and later helping to hide withering bulb foliage. Coarser covers such as English ivy and dwarf periwinkle are ideal companions for bolder bulbs such as daffodils. Shallow-rooted woodland natives such as periwinkle or wintergreen are pretty and happy growing beneath azaleas and rhododendrons.

GROUND COVERS AS PROBLEM-SOLVERS

You can solve, or at least alleviate, many of your toughest landscaping problems by choosing appropriate ground covers. Among them are many 'specialists' that provide tailor-made solutions to specific problems.

Dry sites: In almost any climate dry spots can pose problems to the home owner and gardener. Even in wet seasons, spots beneath overhangs and heavily foliaged trees may remain dry. Water is quickly lost from sun-baked slopes and runs through sandy soil. Where soil is dry due to soil, sun exposure, or climate, drought-tolerant ground covers are often the solution.

In arid climates, you can often forego the need for regular irrigation if you choose the right plants. Drought-resistant plants are a blessing in drought years in any climate when water is in especially short supply.

In some areas of the West, oak root fungus flourishes in irrigated soil, often killing trees and other plants. In these areas, drought-resistant plants won't need watering and they won't be prey to the deadly fungus.

Be aware, however, that all ground covers—even drought-tolerant ones—require regular watering through their first year, or until they are established. And during prolonged drought, some may require occasional watering.

Shady spots: Shady spots on your property are often troublesome spots because most plants won't grow in shade. Lawn grasses fare poorly beneath heavily foliaged trees or on the shaded north side of the house. Keeping these areas attractive becomes a challenge, but you don't have to settle for a lot of bare ground if you want to have beautiful shade trees.

Since many ground covers are woodland natives that are adapted to growing beneath the shade of trees and shrubs, they are naturals for decorating otherwise bare ground in the shady areas of your property. Use the list of shade-loving ground covers on page 14 to help you make a good selection.

Aaron's beard (*Hypericum calycinum*) requires less care than a lawn and tolerates adverse conditions. Sunny yellow flowers, shown below, are borne all summer long.

Trailing lantana (*Lantana montevidensis*) can be used to prevent soil erosion on steep slopes.

Pachysandra (*Pachysandra terminalis*) is ideal for beautifying a shady setting.

Bush morning-glory (*Convolvulus cneorum*) is fire-retardant and drought-tolerant. Flowers are showy through spring and summer.

The branches and foliage of trees and shrubs that cast shade often also act as umbrellas that deflect rain from reaching the ground below. Tree roots may also be close to the soil's surface, taking a lion's share of whatever moisture reaches the soil. (Alder, evergreen elm, willow, and silver maple are among the biggest troublemakers.) So in many shady spots, you'll have success with ground covers only if you water them regularly or if you choose ones that not only tolerate shade, but also do fairly well in dry soil and can compete successfully with tree roots. (See the list on page 16 of ground covers that compete well with tree and shrub roots.)

Steep slopes: It's a difficult, if not impossible, task to mow grass on a steep slope; but unless deep-rooted plants are planted to anchor the soil, erosion is a real threat. Eroded slopes are not only unsightly, but there may be danger of actual damage to your house or property through loss of soil or through mud slides.

Initial, sound engineering is essential for steep banks; terracing or holding the soil with a retaining wall may be called for. Many ground covers stabilize slopes with their deep roots and surface mass and require little maintenance. Hall's Japanese honeysuckle and Aaron's beard are among many ground covers that can transform a raw, rocky bank into a smooth-looking, verdant extension of the garden. (See the list on page 16 for more such ground covers.)

Wet soil: Poor drainage because of heavy soil or contouring that doesn't allow fast run-off causes woe to many gardeners and home owners. Roots of most garden plants 'drown' because of insufficient oxygen. Of course, regrading the land, installing drainage tiles, or amending the soil to improve drainage are possible solutions; planting ground covers that thrive in damp soil is far easier.

No ground cover is a sure solution for the problem of very poorly draining soil. But, for constantly moist soil, the ground covers listed on page 14 offer attractive and inexpensive solutions.

Fire threat: If you live in an area such as the California chaparral where dry summers pose the threat of serious brush fires, you will be wise to use fire-retardant plants to create buffer zones. The ground covers listed on page 15 are attractive as well as being especially fire-retardant.

Maintenance problems: When compared to a lawn, an established ground cover planting is considered low-maintenance. It requires only routine watering, a yearly fertilizing, and perhaps an annual mowing or pruning, and that's it. Because they require so little care, ground covers are ideal for planting on large properties and on steep slopes where maintenance is difficult, and if you haven't much time or energy to devote to gardening chores.

However, new plantings require as much care as a lawn. For the first year, a new planting demands regular watering. Frequent weeding will be necessary for the first several seasons, depending upon how quickly the plants spread. In the long run, most ground covers cut down on the number of weeds—and the time you'll need to spend weeding—by discouraging seed germination in the shade they create and by crowding them out. Ground covers with dense growth habits are the most successful.

DESIGN BASICS

Ground covers can be used in many ways to enhance the appearance of your yard and garden and to solve many of its landscaping problems. But to have a truly beautiful garden, choosing the ground cover that looks right for the part you have assigned it depends upon considering a plant's texture, color, and seasonal characteristics as well as arranging the planting so that it has a pleasing scale and contours.

Texture: Foliage size, flower size, and the thickness and denseness of bare branches in winter all contribute to the textural appearance of a plant. Fine-textured ground covers, such as the needle-leaved junipers or dainty-leaved thyme, are more restful to look at than the bolder-foliaged plants, such as some varieties of hostas or lily-of-the-valley.

As a general rule, in a large-scale planting fine-textured plants are more successful visually than bold-textured ones and do the best job of unifying a landscape. Bold-textured plants are better used in small areas and as accents.

Also consider whether the texture created by leaf patterns will combine well with other plants when you are choosing a ground cover for a particular location. For instance, the spikey lines of the grassy-leaved liriope will combine well with round-leaved plants but be a monotonous repetition of similar lines if planted near a lawn.

Irish and Scotch moss and baby's-tears make dense, fine-textured mats, beautiful at close range or at a distance. Thyme and woolly yarrow make slightly looser, fine-textured mats. 'Wheeler's Dwarf' pittosporum, Japanese spurge, and sweet woodruff each has a different scale but a distinctive starlike texture formed by whorls of foliage. Lily-turf, mondo grass, daylily, and blue fescue vary widely in scale and leaf width but all have a linear pattern like grass. Hostas have broad, often heavily ribbed, wavy-edged, or variegated leaves that grow directly out of the ground and are imposing even at a great distance.

Color: Most ground covers are thought of as foliage plants and used primarily for their greenery. Some offer flowers, berries, or variegated or colored foliage that add bright color to the garden scene.

Ground covers offer many shades of green foliage—including dark green, light green, blue-green, gray-green, and grass-green—and foliage may even be purplish, bronze-hued, or variegated with white or yellow. To use foliage plants most effectively, a careful evaluation of their color impact will give the most satisfactory results. For instance, where you wish to use juniper to border a walkway, there are many varieties to choose from. A bright green one may look cheerful at the nursery, but at home its

color blends right in with the lawn. A silvery gray-green variety provides an eye-catching contrast to the lawn and works much better.

Foliage of some ground covers—notably certain junipers, heavenly bamboo, and wild strawberry—take on darker purplish or reddish hues during the winter. These colors may be a welcome change or distract you into thinking the plants are ill. Other seasonal color highlights are the bright red berries of many hollies and cotoneasters.

Those ground covers that provide vivid flowers may be the most difficult to work into the landscape. The sprinkling of blue flowers of periwinkle works almost anywhere, however the sheets of brilliant color created by verbena, ice plants, or bugleweed, for instance, may clash with or overpower other blooming plants. Used wisely and with caution, such plants create welcome sweeps of color.

Scale: The size of your ground cover planting should fit the scale of your landscape. If you are trying to unite a planting of trees in the front yard, plant a large expanse of ground cover that extends beyond the outer branches of the trees. A little ring of plants beneath a tree gives the tree a top-heavy look—a wide sweep of ground cover beneath provides a substantial-looking footing for the tree and balances its branches.

Similarly a wide driveway demands a bed of ground cover several feet wide. A row of plants would look out of scale while an expanse wider than the driveway itself would be excessive.

Contours: Curves are more interesting than straight lines, so when it comes to designing a bed of ground covers, don't restrict yourself to following straight outlines. A straight walk can be attractively bordered by a curved bed of plants. Similarly, beneath trees and shrubs, try free-form shapes with broad curves. Straight lines in the garden generally create a more formal appearance than curved ones. Each has its place, depending upon the effect you are trying to create in your yard and garden.

Ground covers can create visual harmony when chosen to coordinate with other colors in the garden.

The curving lines of this border of natal plum (*Carissa grandiflora*) and wild strawberry (*Fragaria chiloensis*) are pleasing to look at.

Quick-spreading daylilies (*Hemerocallis* hybrids) adapt to constantly moist soil.

Despite dry conditions, garden verbena (*Verbena peruviana*) blooms from spring to fall.

Barren strawberry (*Waldsteinia fragarioides*) thrives in shade in woodland settings.

Ground Cover Landscape Use Lists

Moist Soil

Few plants survive in soggy soils with poor drainage. These are the best ground covers for moist soils with adequate drainage.

		Zones
Aegopodium podagraria	Goutweed	3-9
Campanula poscharskyana	Serbian Bellflower	3-10
Convallaria majalis	Lily-of-the-Valley	3-10
Euonymus fortunei radicans	Wintercreeper	4-8
Galium odoratum	Sweet Woodruff	4-10
Hemerocallis hybrids	Daylily	2-10
Herniaria glabra	Rupturewort	6-10
Hosta sp.	Hosta	3-9
Lonicera japonica 'Halliana'	Hall's Japanese Honeysuckle	4-10
Pachysandra terminalis	Japanese Spurge	4-9
Paxistima	Paxistima	5-9
Soleirolia soleirolii	Baby's-Tears	8-10

Drought-Tolerant Ground Covers

These plants survive with a minimum amount of water, an important consideration in regions with dry-summer climates.

		Zones
Abelia x grandiflora 'Prostrata'	Prostrate Abelia	6-10
Achillea tomentosa	Woolly Yarrow	3-7

Drought-Tolerant Ground Covers (continued)

		Zones
Aizoaceae sp.	Ice Plant	8-10
Arctostaphylos uva-ursi	Kinnikinick	2-8
Arctotheca calendula	African Daisy, Cape Weed	9-10
Baccharis pilularis	Dwarf Coyote Brush	8-10
Ceanothus sp.	California Lilac	8-10
Cistus sp.	Rock Rose	8-10
Convolvulus cneorum	Bush Morning-Glory	8-10
Coprosma x kirkii	Creeping Coprosma	9-10
Cotoneaster sp.	Cotoneaster	5-10
Cytisus x kewensis	Kew Broom	6-9
Gazania sp.	African Daisy, Gazania	9-10
Genista lydia	Lydia Broom	6-9
Hypericum calycinum	Aaron's Beard	5-10
Iberis sempervirens	Evergreen Candytuft	3-10
Juniperus sp.	Juniper	2-10
Lantana montevidensis	Trailing Lantana	7-10
Myoporum parvifolium	Prostrate Myoporum	9-10
Polygonum sp.	Knotweed	4-10
Rosmarinus officinalis 'Lockwood de Forest'	Trailing Rosemary	7-10
Sedum sp.	Sedum	3-10
Thymus sp.	Creeping Thyme	3-10
Verbena peruviana	Garden Verbena	8-10
Vinca sp.	Periwinkle	5-10

Shade-Tolerant Ground Covers

These are the best ground covers to plant in the shade of trees or along the north side of your house.

		Zones
Aegopodium podagraria	Goutweed	3-9
Ajuga reptans	Carpet Bugle	4-10
Arenaria verna	Irish Moss, Moss Sandwort, Scotch Moss	3-9
Campanula poscharskyana	Serbian Bellflower	3-10
Euonymus fortunei radicans	Wintercreeper	4-8
Galium odoratum	Sweet Woodruff	4-10
Hedera helix	English Ivy	5-10
Hosta sp.	Plantain Lily	3-9
Hypericum calycinum	Aaron's Beard	5-10
Laurentia fluviatilis	Blue Star Creeper	9-10
Liriope sp.	Lilyturf	5-10
Ophiopogon sp.	Mondo Grass	5-10
Pachysandra terminalis	Japanese Spurge	4-9
Paxistima sp.	Paxistima	5-9
Sagina subulata	Irish Moss, Moss Sandwort, Scotch Moss	3-9
Sarcococca hookerana humilis	Sweet Box	7-10
Soleirolia soleirolii	Baby's-Tears	8-10
Taxus baccata 'Repandens'	Spreading English Yew	6-9
Vinca sp.	Periwinkle	5-10
Waldsteinia fragarioides	Barren Strawberry	4-9

English ivy (*Hedera helix*) looks elegant in an expansive setting, where it fills in quickly.

Where the climate is hot and dry, trailing African daisy (*Osteospermum fruticosum*) will cover large areas and require little care.

Trailing rosemary (*Rosmarinus officinalis* 'Lockwood de Forest') combines beauty, fragrance, and fire-retardant qualities.

Ground Covers For Large Areas

These plants form attractive uniform carpets over large areas.

	Zones
Abelia x grandiflora 'Prostrata' Prostrate Abelia	6-10
Aegopodium podagraria Goutweed	3-9
Ajuga reptans Bugleweed	4-10
Arctostaphylos uva-ursi Kinnikinick	2-8
Arctotheca calendula African Daisy, Cape Weed	9-10
Baccharis pilularis Dwarf Coyote Brush	8-10
Berberis thunbergii 'Crimson Pygmy' Crimson Pygmy Japanese Barberry	4-9
Calluna vulgaris Scotch Heather	4-7
Carissa grandiflora Natal Plum	10
Ceanothus California Lilac	8-10
Ceratostigma plumbaginoides Dwarf Plumbago	6-9
Chamaemelum nobile Roman Chamomile	7-10
Cistus sp. Rock Rose	8-10
Convallaria majalis Lily-of-the-Valley	3-9
Coprosma x kirkii Creeping Coprosma	9-10
Cotoneaster (prostrate species) Cotoneaster	5-10
Cytisus x kewensis Kew Broom	6-9
Duchesnia indica Indian Strawberry	5-10
Erica carnea Spring Heath	4-8

Ground Covers For Large Areas
(continued)

	Zones
Euonymus fortunei radicans Wintercreeper	4-8
Fragaria chiloensis Wild Strawberry	4-8
Gazania sp. African Daisy, Gazania	9-10
Genista lydia Lydia Broom	6-9
Hedera helix English Ivy	5-10
Hemerocallis hybrids Daylily	2-10
Hosta sp. Hosta	3-9
Hypericum calycinum Aaron's Beard	5-10
Ilex sp. Holly	6-10
Juniperus sp. Juniper	2-10
Lantana montevidensis Trailing Lantana	9-10
Liriope sp. Lilyturf, Mondo Grass	5-10
Lonicera japonica 'Halliana' Hall's Japanese Honeysuckle	4-10
Mahonia repens Creeping Mahonia	4-10
Myoporum parvifolium Prostrate Myoporum	9-10
Ophiopogon sp. Mondo Grass	5-10
Osteospermum fruticosum Freeway Daisy, Trailing African Daisy	8-10
Pachysandra terminalis Japanese Spurge	4-9
Polygonum sp. Knotweed	4-10
Pyracantha sp. Firethorn	7-10
Rosmarinus officinalis 'Lockwood de forest' Trailing Rosemary	7-10
Sarcococca hookerana humilis Sweet Box	7-10

Ground Covers For Large Areas
(continued)

	Zones
Taxus baccata 'Repandens' Spreading English Yew	6-9
Trachelospermum sp. Star Jasmine	7-10
Verbena peruviana Garden Verbena	8-10
Vinca sp. Periwinkle	5-10
Waldsteinia fragarioides Barren Strawberry	4-9

Fire-Retardant Ground Covers

These plants do not burn easily and can be used to create a buffer zone between your property and areas that are potential fire hazards.

	Zones
Aizoaceae sp. Ice Plant	8-10
Baccharis pilularis Dwarf Coyote Brush	8-10
Cistus sp. Rock Rose	8-10
Convolvulus cneorum Bush Morning-Glory	8-10
Gazania sp. African Daisy, Gazania	9-10
Myoporum parvifolium Prostrate Myoporum	9-10
Rosmarinus officinalis 'Lockwood de Forest' Trailing Rosemary	7-10
Sedum sp. Sedum	3-10

Kinnikinick (*Arctostaphylos uva-ursi*)

Carpet bugle (*Ajuga reptans*)

Roman chamomile (*Chamaemelum nobile*)

Ground Covers for Erosion Control

These plants have strong root systems that bind soil and help prevent erosion on sloping land.

		Zones
Abelia x grandiflora 'Prostrata'	Prostrate Abelia	6-10
Arctostaphylos uva-ursi	Kinnikinick	2-8
Arctotheca calendula	African Daisy, Capeweed	9-10
Baccharis pilularis	Dwarf Coyote Brush	8-10
Calluna vulgaris	Scotch Heather	4-7
Ceanothus sp.	California Lilac	8-10
Cistus sp.	Rock Rose	8-10
Convolvulus cneorum	Bush Morning-Glory	8-10
Coprosma x kirkii	Creeping Coprosma	9-10
Cotoneaster sp.	Cotoneaster	5-10
Erica carnea	Spring Heath	4-8
Euonymus fortunei radicans	Wintercreeper	4-8
Gazania sp.	African Daisy, Gazania	9-10
Hedera helix	English Ivy	5-10
Hemerocallis hybrids	Daylily	7-10
Hypericum calycinum	Aaron's Beard	5-10
Juniperus sp.	Juniper	2-10
Lantana montevidensis	Trailing Lantana	9-10
Lonicera japonica 'Halliana'	Hall's Japanese Honeysuckle	4-10
Myoporum parvifolium	Prostrate Myoporum	9-10
Osteospermum fruticosum	Freeway Daisy, Trailing African Daisy	8-10
Polygonum sp.	Knotweed	4-10
Rosmarinus officinalis 'Lockwood de Forest'	Trailing Rosemary	7-10
Vinca sp.	Periwinkle	5-10

Fast-Growing Ground Covers

These are plants that will cover the ground quickly.

		Zones
Aizoaceae sp.	Ice Plant	8-10
Ajuga reptans	Carpet Bugle	4-10
Arctotheca calendula	African Daisy	9-10
Baccharis pilularis	Dwarf Coyote Brush	8-10
Ceanothus sp.	California Lilac	8-10
Chamaemelum nobile	Roman Chamomile	7-10
Cotoneaster sp.	Cotoneaster	5-10
Euonymus fortunei radicans	Wintercreeper	4-8
Fragaria chiloensis	Wild Strawberry	4-8
Gazania sp.	African Daisy, Gazania	9-10
Lonicera japonica 'Halliana'	Hall's Japanese Honeysuckle	4-10
Osteospermum fruticosum	Freeway Daisy, Trailing African Daisy	8-10
Polygonum sp.	Knotwood	4-10
Sedum sp.	Sedum	3-10
Vinca sp.	Periwinkle	5-10

Ground Covers That Compete Well With Tree and Shrub Roots

These plants have vigorous root systems that can compete for water and nutrients with greedy tree and shrub roots.

		Zones
Duchesnia indica	Indian Strawberry	5-10
Euonymus fortunei radicans	Wintercreeper	4-8

Ground Covers That Complete Well With Tree and Shrub Roots (continued)

		Zones
Hedera helix	English Ivy	5-10
Hemerocallis hybrids	Daylily	2-10
Hypericum calycinum	Aaron's Beard	5-10
Liriope sp.	Lilyturf	5-10
Ophiopogon sp.	Mondo Grass	5-10
Pachysandra terminalis	Japanese Spurge	4-9
Paxistima sp.	Paxistima	5-9
Polygonum sp.	Knotweed	4-10
Sarcococca hookerana humilis	Sweet Box	7-10
Vinca sp.	Periwinkle	5-10

Ground Covers That Tolerate Light Foot Traffic

These plants are not damaged if walked on occasionally; ideal for use between stepping stones or along walkways.

		Zones
Achillea tomentosa	Woolly Yarrow	3-9
Arenaria verna	Irish Moss, Moss Sandwort, Scotch Moss	3-9
Chamaemelum nobile	Roman Chamomile	5-10
Duchesnia indica	Indian Strawberry	5-10
Fragaria chiloensis	Wild Strawberry	4-8
Herniaria glabra	Rupturewort	6-10
Laurentia fluviatilis	Blue Star Creeper	9-10
Sagina subulata	Irish Moss, Moss Sandwort, Scotch Moss	3-9
Soleirolia soleirolii	Baby's-Tears	8-10
Vinca minor	Dwarf Periwinkle	5-10

Scotch heather (*Calluna vulgaris*)

Wild strawberry (*Fragaria chiloensis*)

African daisy (*Gazania* sp.)

Ground Covers by Flowering Seasons

	Zones	Flower Colors	Spring	Summer	Fall
Abelia x grandiflora 'Prostrata' — Prostrate Abelia	6-10	White-pink		■	
Achillea tomentosa — Woolly Yarrow	3-9	Canary-yellow	■		
Aizoaceae sp. — Ice Plant	8-10	Varied	■	■	■
Ajuga reptans — Carpet Bugle	4-10	Blue, pink, white	■		
Arctotheca calendula — African Daisy, Cape Weed	8-10	Varied	■	■	
Bougainvillea sp. — Bougainvillea	9-10	Varied		■	
Calluna vulgaris — Scotch Heather	4-7	Varied		■	■
Campanula poscharskyana — Serbian Bellflower	3-10	Blue		■	
Ceanothus sp. — California Lilac	8-10	Blue, lavender		■	
Ceratostigma plumbaginoides — Dwarf Plumbago	6-9	Blue		■	
Chamaemelum nobile — Roman Chamomile	5-10	Yellow		■	
Cistus sp. — Rock Rose	8-10	White		■	
Convallaria majalis — Lily-of-the-Valley	3-9	White	■		
Convolvulus cneorum — Bush Morning-Glory	8-10	White-pink		■	
Cotoneaster sp. — Cotoneaster	5-10	White to pinkish		■	
Cytisus x kewensis — Kew Broom	6-9	Yellow		■	
Duchesnia indica — Indian Strawberry	5-10	Yellow		■	
Erica carnea — Spring Heath	4-8	White, red, pink	■		
Fragaria chiloensis — Wild Strawberry	4-8	White		■	
Galium odoratum — Sweet Woodruff	4-10	White	■		
Gardenia jasminoides 'Radicans' — Miniature Gardenia	8-10	White		■	
Gazania sp. — African Daisy, Gazania	9-10	Varied	■		■

	Zones	Flower Colors	Spring	Summer	Fall
Genista lydia — Lydia Broom	6-9	Yellow	■		
Hemerocallis hybrids — Daylily	2-10	Varied		■	
Hosta sp. — Plantain Lily	3-7	Lavender, white		■	
Hypericum calycinum — Aaron's Beard	5-10	Yellow		■	
Iberis sempervirens — Evergreen Candytuft	3-10	White	■		
Lantana montevidensis — Trailing Lantana	9-10	Varied	■	■	
Laurentia fluviatilis — Blue Star Creeper	9-10	Blue	■	■	
Liriope sp. — Lilyturf	5-10	Blue-violet		■	
Lonicera japonica 'Halliana' — Hall's Japanese Honeysuckle	4-10	White to yellow	■	■	
Ophiopogon sp. — Mondo Grass	5-10	Blue-violet		■	
Osteospermum fruticosum — Freeway Daisy, Trailing African Daisy	8-10	Varied	■		■
Polygonum sp. — Knotweed	4-10	White		■	
Potentilla tabernaemontanii — Spring Cinquefoil	4-10	Yellow	■	■	■
Pyracantha sp. — Firethorn	6-10	White	■		
Rosmarinus officinalis 'Lockwood de Forest' — Trailing Rosemary	7-10	Blue	■		■
Sarcococca hookerana humilis — Sweet Box	7-10	White	■		
Sedum sp. — Sedum	3-10	Varied		■	
Thymus sp. — Creeping Thyme	3-10	Purplish-white		■	
Trachelospermum jasminoides — Star Jasmine	8-10	White		■	
Verbena peruviana — Garden Verbena	8-10	Pink	■	■	■
Vinca sp. — Periwinkle	5-10	Blue	■	■	■
Waldsteinia fragarioides — Barren Strawberry	4-9	Yellow	■		

Guide to Top-Rated Ground Covers

The ground cover plants described here qualify as top-rated plants because they are widely available from nurseries and garden centers, and because they are excellent performers in the regions where they are available. Of the several hundred plants used as ground covers in North America, only these top-rated ones meet these criteria. Among them are vines, dwarf or prostrate shrubs, perennials, succulents, and herbs.

Encyclopedia entries: Plant descriptions are arranged alphabetically by the botanical name of the plant genus. The most popular common names of each plant are given in larger, bolder type. The hardiness zones where the plant is adapted and the average height and spread of mature plants are given.

Evergreen plants are ones that retain their leaves all year; deciduous ones lose their foliage in winter. Woody plants have twigs and stems that live through the winter. Herbaceous plants usually die to the ground in fall, but regrow in spring.

Each entry discusses the plant's appearance and gives landscape use suggestions. Recommendations for planting and care are given and if any disease or insect problems are severe, they are mentioned. In some cases, particularly suitable varieties are mentioned.

Botanical names: This encyclopedia uses botanical names, since common names are often regional, highly variable, and may refer to several different plants. The Name Cross-Reference Guide on page 63 matches common names with their correct botanical names.

At left: Ground cover plantings in large areas create a luxurious setting without creating a closed-in feeling.

Natal plum (*Carissa grandiflora*)

Roman chamomile (*Chamaemelum nobile*)

Scotch heather (*Calluna vulgaris*)

Indian strawberry (*Duchesnia indica*)

Low-maintenance prostrate abelia (*Abelia x grandiflora* 'Prostrata') is highly effective for covering slopes.

Perfect between stepping stones, woolly yarrow (*Achillea tomentosa*) tolerates light foot traffic.

Variegated forms of goutweed (*Aegopodium podagraria*) brighten up shady spots.

Abelia x grandiflora 'Prostrata'
Prostrate Abelia
Zones: 6-10. To 18-24 inches tall, spreads to 4 feet.
Evergreen or semideciduous.
Flowering.

Prostrate abelia is a spreading form of glossy abelia. Like its larger form, this widely used dwarf shrub creates a mass of rich, shiny greenery. The inch-long leaves emerge bronze, maturing to dark green. Small clusters of bell-shaped white or pink-tinged flowers, 3/4 inch long, appear throughout summer and sometimes bloom into fall.

Prostrate abelia is hardy to 0°F. In mildest areas, foliage remains lush year-round; in cold areas, plants are semideciduous, losing most of their foliage.

This low-maintenance plant is excellent for covering slopes. Once established it requires little water. Pruning or shearing encourages compactness. Space prostrate abelia plants 3-1/2 feet apart in ordinary garden soil. Prefers full sun but does well in partial shade.

Achillea tomentosa
Woolly Yarrow
Zones: 3-9. To 6-9 inches.
Evergreen. Flowering.

As with most yarrows, this plant is delicate-looking, but tough. When out of bloom, it creates a ground-hugging mass from 1 to 3 inches tall. These low clumps of soft-textured foliage make a long-lasting ground cover that endures adverse growing conditions and occasional light foot traffic.

Leaves are tiny, finely divided, 4 inches long, and gray-green with a soft, feathery texture. From spring through summer, woolly yarrow produces numerous dense, flat, 2- to 3-inch-wide clusters of tiny yellow flowers on top of 6- to 9-inch-tall stems.

This care-free plant thrives on neglect, grows in any type of soil, and prefers full sun. Watering is necessary only when plants show signs of stress. Will look best if flowering stems are clipped or mowed back after the blooming season. Old or ragged foliage may also be cut back in spring. May be propagated by dividing clumps. Space new plants 6 to 12 inches apart. Woolly yarrow is hardy to -40°°F.

Aegopodium podagraria
Goutweed, Bishop's Weed
Zones: 3-9. To 6-12 inches, spreads to 4 feet.
Deciduous. Flowering.

Goutweed spreads aggressively by creeping underground stems, making it a good choice for erosion control in problem spots but an unwise choice for well-tended gardens. It may be safely planted in areas where pavement or walls restrict its wandering roots. Thriving in either moist or dry soil, sun or shade, goutweed can solve many problems as long as it doesn't become a problem weed itself.

The light green leaves are coarsely divided into oval leaflets and grow on stems 6 to 12 inches tall. For about a month in late spring or early summer, dainty white flower heads stand above the foliage. A variety with white-rimmed leaves, 'Variegatum', is the most popular form and is eye-catching in shady spots. It is slightly less invasive than the green form.

Space goutweed plants 2 feet apart in poor or average soil; plants grow too vigorously in rich soil. Goutweed can be kept low and neat by mowing it two or three times a season with a rotary mower with blades set high. Though tops die to the ground with first frost; roots are hardy to -40°F.

Aizoaceae
Ice Plant Family
Zones: 8-10. To 1-24 inches, spreads to 12 inches.
Evergreen succulents.
Flowering.

This large family encompasses several genera of creeping succulent plants that make excellent showy ground covers in warm or arid climates. They are valued as fire-retardant, drought-tolerant plants that are able to grow under adverse conditions such as dry soil or in reach of salt spray. (See chart.)

Members of the ice plant family (*Aizoaceae*) thrive on neglect and are drought-tolerant. In warm climates, their masses of showy flowers add brilliant color to the most difficult sites. Pig's face (*Carpobrotus chilensis*), above left; rosea ice plant (*Drosanthemum floribundum*), top right; trailing ice plant (*Lampranthus spectabilis*), lower right.

Ice Plants

Botanical Name/Common Name	Zones	Size	Plant Description	Comments
Carpobrotus chilensis (*Mesembryanthemum aequilaterale*) Pig's Face	9-10	To 12-18 in.	Fast-growing with succulent, 2-in., 3-sided leaves. Rose-purple flowers in midsummer.	Good for stabilizing shifting sand. Do not overwater. Space 12 to 18 in. apart for a quick cover.
C. edulis (*Mesembryanthemum edule*) Hottentot Fig	9-10	To 12-18 in.	Fast-growing with succulent, 5-in., 3-sided, curved leaves. Light yellow to pale pink flowers in midsummer.	Fruit edible but not very tasty. Same uses and culture as *C. chilensis*.
Cephalophyllum 'Red Spike' (*Cylindrophyllum speciosum*) Red Spike Ice Plant	8-10	To 3-5 in.	Striking red leaves are small, spikelike. Cerise flowers in late winter and early spring.	Attracts bees. Space 6-12 in. apart.
Delosperma 'Alba' White Trailing Ice Plant	9-10	To 6-7 in.	Fast-growing trailing stems root as they spread. Triangular leaves are 1 in. long. Small white flowers not very showy but attract bees.	Good slope stabilizer. Space 12 in. apart for quick cover.
Drosanthemum floribundum Rosea Ice Plant	9-10	To 6 in.	Leaves narrow and dense, crystalline texture. Wide-spreading stems. Bright pink flowers, late spring to early summer.	Best ice plant for erosion control on steep slopes. Will trail and spill over walls. Space 12 in. apart.
D. hispidum	9-10	To 2 ft	Leaves similar to *D. floribundum* but has a more mounding habit. Purple flowers in late spring and early summer.	Does not bind soil as well as rosea ice plant. Space 12 in. apart.
Lampranthus aurantiacus Bush Ice Plant	9-10	To 10-15 in.	Erect habit with gray-green, 1-in., 3-sided leaves. Flowers 1-1/2 to 2 in. wide, bright yellow or orange.	Brilliant colored flowers. Cut back for compact growth. Excellent for use in coastal climates. Space 8 in. apart.
L. ficicaulis Redondo Creeper	9-10	To 3 in.	Slow-growing with small, fine-textured foliage. Small pink flowers in early spring.	Good small-scale ground cover. Space plants 12 in. apart.
L. productus Purple Ice Plant	9-10	To 15 in.	Upright habit with bronze-tipped, gray-green leaves. Bright purple flowers in late winter and spring.	Space plants 12-18 in. apart.
L. spectabilis Trailing Ice Plant	9-10	To 15 in.	Upright habit with gray-green leaves. Masses of red, purple, or pink flowers in spring.	Most spectacular blooming *Lampranthus*. An unbroken carpet of color at peak bloom. Space 12-18 in. apart.

Purple-leaved forms of bugleweed (*Ajuga reptans*) create pleasing color-contrast to green-leaved plants.

Creating a dense mat of glossy foliage, kinnikinick (*Arctostaphylos uva-ursi*) is a choice plant for erosion control in dry and difficult sites.

Tolerant of drought and heat, cape weed (*Arctotheca calendula*) adds dramatic color to the landscape, flowering intermittently throughout the year.

Ajuga reptans
Bugleweed, Carpet Bugle

Zones: 4-10. To 2-4 inches, spreads to 3 feet.
Evergreen. Flowering.

Carpet bugle is an all-time favorite ground cover for gardens with rich soil, good drainage, ample moisture, and some shade, where it carpets the ground with a mat of foliage. The oval leaves grow close together along ground-hugging stems. Foliage of the species is dark green and slightly wavy, with prominent veins that give it a quilted look. Some varieties have bronze- or purple-colored foliage; others have green foliage variegated with white, white and pink, or yellow. These form make stunning accent plantings.

In spring and early summer, upright spikes of small, bright bluish-purple flowers appear, growing 5 or 6 inches above the foliage. Some varieties have white or pink flowers.

Bugleweed forms an attractive flat mat that's ideal for decorating the ground beneath trees and shrubs, over a bulb bed, and as a filler used in limited areas such as shaded parking strips. It is unsurpassed for year-round attractiveness in mild climates and for a long season elsewhere.

Carpet bugle spreads rapidly by creeping surface runners, which root to form new plants, quickly filling in a new planting. Space plants 6 to 18 inches apart in average to rich soil. Except in mild-summer climates, some shade is desirable, although plants mildew in too much shade if air circulation is poor. If drainage is poor or if soil is heavy clay, root rot may be a problem.

If ideally situated, bugleweed requires only seasonal clipping of spent flower spikes to look its best. Occasionally, however, small areas may die back and need replanting. After several years, green-leaved seedlings may invade plantings of bugleweed with variegated or colored foliage; these should be weeded out or they will crowd out the original plants. Regular weeding out of these seedlings will make the job be less of a task.

Arctostaphylos uva-ursi
Kinnikinick

Zones: 2-8. To 5-10 inches, spreads to 15 feet.
Evergreen. Flowering.

From the Pacific Northwest to New England and the Maritime Provinces of Canada, this prostrate member of the manzanita genus is an outstanding plant for solving erosion problems. It is particularly useful on steep slopes, in sandy soil, under deciduous oaks, draped over walls, and in areas seldom watered, although unlike most manzanitas it tolerates watering, if soil is well drained.

Leaves, 3/4 to 1 inch long, are glossy, leathery, and bright green. They cover the woody stems, creating a dense mat. In winter, leaves take on a reddish cast. In spring, 1/4-inch-long urn-shaped white or pinkish flowers appear; they are beautiful on close inspection but too small to be showy. Flowers are followed in fall by bright red berries, 1/4 inch across, which last through winter or until birds have eaten them.

Set gallon-size kinnikinick plants 3 feet apart. Rooted cuttings from flats can be set at 6-inch intervals and thinned later. Thrives in any type of soil; in sun or partial shade. Because its growth rate is slow, heavy mulching is recommended to help keep weeds under control until kinnikinick covers the ground completely.

Arctotheca calendula
Cape Weed

Zones: 9-10. To 12 inches, spreads to 1-1/2 feet.
Evergreen. Flowering.

Coarse at close range, from a distance masses of cape weed in flower create sensational color over a long season. It is a dependable evergreen cover when not blooming and is one of the easiest covers to establish on both banks or level areas with good drainage.

Leaves are gray-green and woolly underneath, rough-hairy above. Intermittently throughout the year, cape weed produces bright yellow 2-inch "daisies," which open fully only in sunny weather, closing at night. In spring, flowering can be so profuse as to hide the foliage. Cape weed spreads by runners and can reach up to 1-1/2 feet wide in a single season.

Plant in early fall, spacing plants about 15 inches apart for complete coverage in a season. Any garden soil is acceptable; prefers full sun. Mowing or clipping annually makes for a dense, even cover. Once established, cape weed needs little water and withstands intense heat. Leaves are damaged at about 25°F, but plants recover quickly.

Arenaria verna, Sagina subulata
Irish Moss, Scotch Moss, Moss Sandwort
Zones: 3-9. To 1-3 inches, spreads to 6 inches.
Evergreen. Flowering.

Two different plants are called Irish moss: *Arenaria verna (A. caespitosa)* and *Sagina subulata*. Purists label the latter Irish moss and the former moss sandwort. But nurseries sell both as Irish moss; and in size, appearance, and requirements, they are almost identical. Both have light green forms—*A.v.* 'Aurea' and *S. s.* 'Aurea'—that are called Scotch moss. Though Irish moss looks delicate, these two species are among the toughest and most cold-hardy ground covers.

Not true mosses, but diminutive flowering plants with mosslike texture, Irish moss has tiny leaves of a rich green and those of Scotch moss are bright yellow-green. Both bear tiny white flowers, *Sagina* singly and *Arenaria* in small clusters, in summer.

These elegant ground covers are very decorative as lawn substitutes in small areas and where a very fine texture is desired. They make excellent fillers around low shrubs and between stepping stones, and are beautiful among large rocks, ferns, and other woodland plants. They fit perfectly into Oriental gardens.

To plant, cut small plugs from a flat and space 6 inches apart. Thrives in sun or shade; prefers rich soil and regular watering. Plants spread rapidly, and self-sow prolifically. They tend to form mounds, a habit which can be controlled by cutting out narrow strips.

Scotch moss (*Arenaria verna* 'Aurea') is a rugged and cold-hardy plant that makes a maintenance-free lawn substitute.

Widely adapted Irish moss (*Arenaria verna*) forms a thick deep green carpet that resembles moss.

Dwarf coyote brush (*Baccharis pilularis*) quickly creates a bright green cover even under the toughest growing conditions.

A planting of crimson pygmy Japanese barberry (*Berberis thunbergii* 'Crimson Pygmy') will fill in to create a colorful knee-high barrier.

Bougainvillea (*Bougainvillea* sp.) make colorful companions for evergreen ground covers, which provide protection from frost.

Baccharis pilularis

Dwarf Coyote Brush, Dwarf Chaparral Broom

Zones: 8-10. To 6-24 inches, spreads to 10 feet.
Evergreen.

This fast-growing native to the California Coast has a cast-iron constitution and adapts to inland areas, even thriving in the high desert. In much of the West it creates a dependable green mounding cover for areas where soil is very poor, dry, or wet and where heat is intense. Dwarf coyote brush is becoming a common sight on banks along freeways and in areas where lawns once grew in home landscapes, where it conserves water and maintenance effort. It is especially useful for controlling erosion on steep slopes.

Plants have a mounding habit. Leaves are toothed, 1/2 to 1 inch long, dense and bright green. Flowers are inconspicuous. Because female plants produce messy, white cottony seeds, male plants are most commonly available at nurseries.

Plant in full sun in poor to average soil. Space plants 2 to 4 feet apart. To obtain densest growth, annual pruning or shearing before rapid growth begins in spring is recommended.

'Twin Peaks #2', widely available, grows 6 to 12 inches high and spreads to 6 feet or more. 'Pigeon Point' grows about 2 feet tall and spreads to 9 feet wide. Its foliage is large and bright green.

Berberis thunbergii 'Crimson Pygmy'

Crimson Pygmy Japanese Barberry

Zones: 4-9. To 18 inches, spreads to 2 feet.
Deciduous. Flowering.

This woody ground cover is a purple-leaved dwarf form of Japanese barberry, a popular hedge plant. 'Crimson Pygmy' has purple-red leaves in sun, green leaves in shade. It is also sold as 'Atropurpurea Nana', 'Little Beauty', and 'Little Gem'.

'Crimson Pygmy' grows at a moderate rate to 18 inches high, spreading to 2 feet wide. Roundish leaves,

3/4 inch long, have brilliant red color in fall. In spring 'Crimson Pygmy' has clusters of small, waxy yellow flowers, followed by bright red berries in fall.

A versatile shrub, it thrives in sun or shade, good soil or poor, and is hardy to −20°F. Space plants 15 inches apart.

The thorny plants make a useful low barrier planting or bank cover. Combine them with creeping junipers on a slope for nice color and foliage contrast.

Other dwarf varieties of Japanese barberry are available: 'Dobold' is identical to 'Crimson Pygmy' except leaves are bright green. 'Rose Glow' has brilliant red new growth that ages to deep red with pinkish-white variegation.

Bougainvillea

Bougainvillea

Zones: 9-10. To 2-3 feet, spreads to 6 feet.
Evergreen. Flowering.

This brilliant subtropical vine can be used on sunny banks to create a strikingly colorful ground cover that blooms most of the year. Bougainvillea "flowers" are actually brilliantly colored bracts that surround the true flowers. They appear in great colorful masses throughout the warm months. The leaves are pointed, nearly oval, to 2 inches or longer.

In areas where it is borderline cold-hardy, bougainvillea often survives in sheltered, sunny spots, especially if it can be brought through its first winter successfully. It is often planted with a flowerless ground cover such as English ivy to provide additional protection from cold.

Starting bougainvillea is tricky, since the roots resent being disturbed. It's best to plant in spring, just when the ground has warmed. Be extremely careful not to disturb the rootball, keeping all the soil intact. If the can is metal or wood fiber, you can carefully cut slits in the sides and bottom for maximum drainage and plant the entire can, which soon deteriorates. Space plants 3 feet apart in full sun. If a bougainvillea plant is happily situated, it grows rapidly.

Fertilize from early spring through midsummer and mulch around the plants in summer. While plants are tough and resilient once established, they may be bothered by aphids, mealybugs, caterpillars, and scale. If plants produce strong vertical growth, it should be removed to encourage spreading.

The following varieties all have a low and mounding habit, best for ground cover plantings: 'Crimson Jewel' has crimson-red flowers and 'La Jolla' has fluorescent-red flowers. 'Hawaii' has red flowers, creamy-margined leaves, and is especially hardy.

Calluna vulgaris
Scotch Heather

Zones: 4-7. To 2-3 feet, spreads to 2 feet.
Evergreen. Flowering.

This true heather, and one of the choicest, is widely used as a ground cover in both European and North American gardens. Plants vary from low, twiggy mounding forms suitable for ground covers to larger forms used as specimens, in borders, or as covers for large areas. Great masses of tiny pink, lavender, purple, or pure white flowers cover Scotch heather during mid- and late summer.

Leaves are tiny, overlapping juniperlike needles, varying from gray to russet, chartreuse, and deep green, depending on the variety. The foliage of some varieties colors in autumn. Flowers are 1/4 inch long, bell-shaped, and arranged along the branch tips. They are used as dried and fresh cut flowers.

Set plants of dwarf varieties 1 to 2 feet apart, planting in early spring. Full sun encourages profuse blooming, but partial shade is acceptable. Infertile soil is best, since rich soil makes plants leggy and unattractive. Prune or shear in early spring, before plants have begun growing, to tidy up plants and encourage heavy new growth. Hardy to −20°F.

There are over 70 varieties of heather available, many of them dwarf and suitable for ground cover use.

Scotch heather (*Calluna vulgaris*), shown above and below, forms mounds of upright branches that are spectacular during mid- and late summer when they are covered with masses of bright blooms.

Although fragile in appearance, Serbian bellflower (*Campanula poscharskyana*) is tough and rugged, tolerating cold, heat, and some drought.

Dwarf varieties of natal plum (*Carissa grandiflora*) make a knee-high barrier planting along a walkway that is brightened most of the year with white flowers and showy fruit (shown below).

Campanula poscharskyana
Serbian Bellflower
Zones: 3-10. To 12 inches, spreads to 4 feet.
Deciduous. Flowering.

This pretty perennial produces star-shaped flowers from spring into summer, often into fall, and looks attractive and dainty in small, partly shaded areas. Though delicate in appearance, it is a rugged plant that withstands temperatures of −35°F as well as some drought and summer heat. It is one of the most enduring flowering ground covers.

Flowers, 1/2 to 1 inch wide, punctuate shaded beds with their star shapes in various shades of lavender-blue over a long season, creating a woodland atmosphere. Stems are long, to around 2 feet, but trail so that the plant is only a few inches high, rarely taller than a foot. Leaves are kidney-shaped, medium green and 1-1/2 inches long, with serrated edges.

Space Serbian bellflower plants 1 to 2 feet apart in spring in partial shade in rich to average soil. Clip dead flowers. Divide clumps every 3 or 4 years.

Carissa grandiflora
Natal Plum
Zone: 10. To 18-24 inches, spreads to 5 feet.
Evergreen. Flowering.

In the warmest areas, especially in seashore gardens where salt spray is a problem, dwarf forms of natal plum make an excellent ground cover or low barrier planting. Two-inch, white, starlike flowers, fragrant as jasmine, appear intermittently throughout the year, followed by edible plumlike fruit. Leaves are dark, glossy, and roundish, up to 3 inches wide, and stems are armed with sharp thorns.

'Green Carpet' and 'Prostrata' are top-rated dwarf varieties excellent for ground cover use. 'Green Carpet' grows 18 inches high and eventually spreads to form a 4-foot-wide mound. It has smaller leaves than 'Prostrata', which reaches 2 feet high and spreads to 5 feet. Unlike slower 'Green Carpet', it grows at a moderate rate. They are hardy to 30°F, but often are grown in gardens in colder areas where warm microclimates protect them from winter cold.

Space natal plum plants 2 feet apart in sun or partial shade. Average to rich soil is preferred. Occasional pruning to shape plants is the only requirement of the easy-to-grow natal plum.

Ceanothus species
California Lilac, Wild Lilac
Zones: 8-10. To 3-36 inches, spreads to 30 feet.
Evergreen. Flowering.

In coastal areas of the West, few prostrate shrubs produce lovelier spring flowers or more satisfactory year-round greenery than does California lilac. Several species and varieties of *Ceonanthus*, a large genus of native California shrubs, are useful for covering large areas that have good drainage and plenty of sun. Bank plantings are best.

Flowers, near white, bright blue, or blue-purple, are in numerous tight clusters. They are fragrant and attract bees. Leaves may vary from round, glossy, and flat (3-inch, bold-textured leaves of *C. griseus horizontalis*) to small and spiny (1-inch, leathery leaves of *C. gloriosus*).

Plants range from around 3 inches high (*C. divergens confusus*) to 3 feet high (*C.* 'Joyce Coulter'). The widest spreader reaches 30 feet (*C. griseus horizontalis* 'Hurricane Point').

California lilac thrives in coastal areas. A few varieties adapt to hot-summer inland areas. Most varieties do not like to be pruned. When grown out of their ideal range or when some of their basic needs are not met, they can be short-lived.

These top-rated varieties are available locally: *C. divergens confusus* (Rincon ceanothus) grows 3 inches high, 3 feet wide; space plants 18 inches apart. *C. gloriosus* (Point Reyes ceanothus) grows 18 inches high, 18 feet wide; space plants 3 to 4 feet apart. *C. g.* 'Anchor Bay' has especially compact growth and *C. g. exaltatus* 'Emily Brown' grows 1-1/2 to 3 feet high, 10 feet wide; space plants 7 to 10 feet apart. *C. g. porrectus* (Mount Vision ceanothus) grows 1 to 3 feet high, spreads to 8 feet wide, or wider; space plants 6 to 8 feet apart. *C. griseus horizontalis* 'Hurricane Point' and 'Yankee Point' are wide spreading; space 4 feet apart, or more, depending upon the situation. *C.* 'Joyce Coulter' grows 3 feet high, 10 to 12 feet wide; space plants 4 to 5 feet apart. *C. maritimus* grows 2-1/2 feet high, 6 feet wide; space plants 2 to 3 feet apart.

Ceratostigma plumbaginoides
Dwarf Plumbago, Leadwort
Zones: 6-9. To 10-12 inches, spreads to 4 feet.
Deciduous. Flowering.

Leadwort is an exceptionally tough ground cover that dies back in winter, then reappears promptly with the return of warm weather. It grows in clumps, and spreads vigorously by underground stems. Brilliant blue flowers in dense clusters appear from midsummer into fall, a time when few other blue flowers are blooming. The round, flat flowers resemble phlox, but their blue color is unique in its intensity.

Leaves are dark green with reddish overtones. In mildest areas, foliage turns red and stays on plants for weeks or months in winter (though plants are best clipped to the ground then).

Space leadwort plants 1 to 2 feet apart in average to rich soil. Thrives in sun or partial shade. It is best used where its invasive, spreading roots can be restrained. Leadwort is hardy to −10°F.

Chamaemelum nobile (Anthemis nobilis)
Roman Chamomile
Zones: 7-10. To 12 inches, spreads to 2 feet.
Evergreen. Flowering.

This favorite source for herb tea (the other herbal chamomile is *Matricaria*) is also one of the oldest known lawn substitutes, used in England since Elizabethan times, or

In arid climates and coastal areas, California lilacs (*Ceanothus* sp.) will spread out over a bank and control erosion effectively.

Leadwort (*Ceratostigma plumbaginoides*) bears pretty, bright blue flowers from midsummer into fall.

Roman chamomile (*Chamaemelum nobile*) bears a profusion of small flowers in summer.

For covering dry, difficult growing sites in mild climates, rock rose (*Cistus* sp.) has no peer.

Lily-of-the-valley (*Convallaria majalis*) thrives in shade. Its lush foliage and charming bell-like flowers are attractive in large or small areas.

Ground morning-glory (*Convolvulus mauritanicus*) has muted gray-green foliage and colorful blossoms that cover plants for a long season.

earlier. One of the few fine-textured ground covers virtually unaffected by foot traffic, it has proven to be the ideal alternative for many gardeners who don't want a high-maintenance grass lawn.

If not walked on and left unclipped, especially in shade, Roman chamomile grows up to a foot high. It makes an attractive medium-height ground cover or border plant that remains relatively attractive during winter months. Clipped, it makes a perfect cover around stepping stones or in larger areas.

Flowers are petalless golden buttons, 1/4 to 1/2 inch wide. They appear through summer months. Less common forms have small daisylike flowers. Grass-green leaves are finely divided, ferny, and fragrant when crushed. They form a low, dense mat in full sun, and can be mowed annually to remove spent flower heads and encourage dense growth.

Space chamomile plants 8 to 12 inches apart. Prefers average to rich soil; tolerates partial shade.

Cistus species
Rock Rose

Zones: 8-10. To 18 inches - 5 feet, spreads to 5 feet.
Evergreen. Flowering.

Rock rose is a top-rated ground cover with white or pink flat flowers that resemble single roses, fragrant foliage, and a fire-retardant nature. It looks its best in the poorest soil with no water in summer. Both its beauty and durability make rock rose an ideal solution for covering inaccessible sunny, dry banks or steep slopes, where a low-maintenance planting is needed.

Rock rose is not fussy about soil but prefers full sun. Space plants 1 to 4 feet apart, depending on the spreading habit of the variety.

There are many varieties ranging in size from 18 inches to 5 feet high and spreading to various widths. These varieties are top-rated as ground covers: *C. crispus*, 18 inches high and wide. *C. x hybridus*, 2 feet high, 5 feet wide. *C. salviifolius*, 2 feet high, 6 feet wide. 'Doris Hibberson', 3 feet high and wide.

Convallaria majalis
Lily-of-the-Valley

Zones: 3-9. To 6-8 inches, spreads to 4 feet.
Deciduous. Flowering.

Lily-of-the-valley is loved for its sprays of delicately scented bell-shaped flowers. Handsome dark-green leaves, about 8 inches high and 2 to 3 inches wide, grow directly from the ground. Flowers appear in late spring, followed by a scattering of red berries in fall. In winter plants die back to the ground, but in spring and summer their lush foliage and attractive blossoms make them choice ground covers.

The plants thrive in full to light shade and can be used to cover large or small areas, such as sections of a woodland garden, areas on north or east sides of houses, or spaces between shrubs. Plants spread rapidly by underground runners, so that a dense mat forms; too invasive for planting near most perennials and annuals, or even lawns.

Plant clumps of underground stems, called pips, 1 to 2 feet apart; or individual pips 4 to 6 inches apart; 1 to 2 inches deep, in partial shade. Average to rich soil is preferred. Does not do well in mild climates. All parts of the plant are toxic, if eaten.

Convolvulus cneorum
Bush Morning-Glory

Zones: 7-10. To 2-4 feet, spreading to 4 feet.
Evergreen. Flowering.

This Mediterranean native is an excellent ground cover for dry hillsides and banks. Silvery foliage, a graceful spreading habit, and white trumpet-shaped blossoms blooming for a long season contribute to this shrub's attractiveness. Its fire-retardant and drought-tolerant qualities are also valuable assets.

Bush morning-glory is hardy to 15°F and like its vining cousins, grows rapidly. Properly situated in full sun, it forms a compact plant that flowers profusely. Blossoms are white tinted with pink and are 1 to 2 inches wide. They appear continuously through spring and summer.

Two- to 3-inch-long leaves are narrow, downy, and silvery.

C. mauritanicus (ground morning-glory), grows 1 to 2 feet high and spreads to 3 feet or wider. Foliage is soft gray-green and flowers are blue. Space both species 2 feet apart. Both tolerate dry soil and prefer full sun.

Coprosma x kirkii
Creeping Coprosma
Zones: 9-10. To 2-3 feet, spreads 3 to 5 feet.
Evergreen.

This rapid-growing, spreading shrub from New Zealand does well in North American gardens only in California, where it is especially valuable for preventing erosion of steep slopes. It is also widely used for seaside plantings because it withstands salt spray and constant wind.

Flowers are inconspicuous, but the light green, narrow 1/2- to 1-inch leaves are exceptionally attractive and remain year round.

Creeping coprosma tolerates poor soil and sun or partial shade. Space 2 feet apart. Hardy to 20°F.

Cotoneaster species
Cotoneaster
Zones: 5-10. To 6-36 inches, spreads to 12 feet.
Deciduous and evergreen.
Flowering.

Many members of this large genus make decorative bank and ground covers. All are tough twiggy shrubs that tolerate poor, dry soils and temperature extremes, and are excellent for erosion control on steep slopes. Most have clusters of small white or pink flowers in spring. All have masses of showy red berries from fall through winter.

Cotoneasters are not fussy about soil and tolerate sun and partial shade. Set plants at 2- to 6-foot intervals, depending upon the natural spread of the species or variety. Prune as needed with clippers. Cotoneasters are susceptible to the bacterial disease fireblight. Top-rated cotoneasters are described in the chart on the next page.

Widely used in California for erosion control on steep banks, creeping coprosma (*Coprosma x kirkii*) grows rapidly and tolerates salt spray and wind.

The dense, matlike growth and wide-spreading habit of bearberry cotoneaster (*Cotoneaster dammeri*) make it ideally suited for covering slopes and banks.

Bearberry cotoneaster (*Cotoneaster dammeri*) creates a soft-textured evergreen cover that's attractive in large areas.

Rock cotoneaster (*Cotoneaster horizontalis*) has orange-red foliage in fall and bounteous red berries that are showy through winter.

Useful also as a cover in small settings, cotoneaster (*Cotoneaster* sp.) adds visual interest to the landscape throughout the year.

Cotoneaster

Botanical Name/Common Name	Zones	Size	Plant Description	Comments
Cotoneaster adpressus praecox **Early Cotoneaster**	5-10	To 2 ft tall. Spreads to 6 ft.	Deciduous shrub. Leaves small, round, shiny dark green with wavy edges, turn brilliant red in fall. Small pink flowers in spring are followed by heavy crop of red berries.	Use for ground cover, on banks, in rock gardens. Exceptionally resistant to fireblight.
C. apiculatus 'Nanus' **Dwarf Cranberry Cotoneaster**	5-10	To 1-1/2 to 2 ft tall.	Dwarf shrub similar to species but evergreen in mild climates.	Well-suited for rock gardens and mound plantings.
C. buxifolius (C. glaucophyllus) **Gray-Leafed Cotoneaster**	7-10	To 1-2 ft tall. Spreads 4-6 ft.	Semievergreen shrub. Branches arching. Leaves oval, gray-green above, white or tan fuzz beneath. Flowers in dense clusters. Berries bright red along branches.	Frequently mislabeled in nurseries. Good for rock gardens, bank covers. Excellent for dry areas.
C. congestus 'Likiang'	6-10	To 3 ft tall.	Evergreen shrub. Compact, low-spreading habit with arching branches. Leaves small, dense, dark green. White flowers in early spring. Small red berries in fall.	Grows well in arid climates. Good for rock gardens.
C. dammeri **Bearberry Cotoneaster**	5-10	To 6-12 in. tall. Spreads to 10 ft.	Evergreen shrub. Prostrate growth habit. Leaves 1 in., oval, bright green above, pale beneath. Flowers white, fairly showy. Brilliant red berries in fall.	Forms dense mat; ground cover. Excellent cascading effect over a wall and among rocks. Will grow in partial shade.
C. d. 'Coral Beauty' **Coral Beauty Cotoneaster**	5-10	To 6-12 in. tall. Spreads to 10 ft.	Evergreen shrub. Similar to species. Leaves small, rich green. Profusion of brilliant coral-colored berries in fall.	Good choice for rock gardens. Trailing growth habit.
C. d. 'Lowfast'	5-10	To 6-12 in. tall. Spreads to 10 ft.	Evergreen shrub. Similar to species. Leaves glossy. White flowers 1/2 in. across. Showy berries are brilliant red.	Grows fast. Excellent ground cover.
C. d. 'Moon Creeper'	5-10	To 6-12 in. tall. Spreads to 10 ft.	Evergreen shrub. Similar to species but lower-growing than most. Forms an even-topped cover.	Less tendency to mound-up where original clumps were planted.
C. d. 'Royal Beauty'	5-10	To 6-12 in. tall. Spreads to 10 ft.	Evergreen shrub. Similar to species. Deep coral-red berries formed early; contrast well with rich, glossy foliage.	Vigorous ground cover, or plant to cascade over wall.
C. horizontalis **Rock Cotoneaster**	5-10	To 3 ft tall. Spreads to 15 ft.	Deciduous shrub. Small, round, dark leaves, glossy green above, pale beneath, turn reddish orange in fall before dropping. Pink flowers in spring. Berries shiny, bright red.	Berries so plentiful, deciduous habit goes unnoticed in winter. Good as low traffic barrier or bank cover.
C. microphyllus **Rock Spray Cotoneaster**	6-10	To 2-3 ft tall. Spreads to 6 ft.	Evergreen shrub. Dense growth. Small dark green leaves. White flowers in spring; bright red berries in fall.	
C. salicifolius 'Herbstfeuer' **(C. s. 'Autumn Fire')** **Willow-Leaf Cotoneaster**	6-10	To 6 in. tall. Spreads to 8 ft.	Evergreen shrub. Branches arching. Leaves narrow, long, dark green above, grayish beneath. White flowers in clusters followed by red berries.	Excellent ground cover for sun or shade.
C. s. 'Repens' **(C. s. 'Repandens')**	6-10	To 2-3 ft tall. Spreads to 8 ft.	Semievergreen shrub. Similar to *C. s.* 'Herbstfeuer'	Very versatile; use as ground cover, on banks, or in hanging basket.

Cytisus x kewensis
Kew Broom

Zones: 6-9. To 12 inches, spreads to 6 feet.
Deciduous. Flowering.

When in full blossom in spring, Kew broom is a mass of alluring color. Its half-inch, sweet-pea flowers, which cover the plant in midspring, are creamy white. When many plants are massed together as a ground cover or planted to cascade gracefully down a bank or over a wall, the display is dazzling.

Though it drops its tiny leaves in fall, Kew broom has the effect of an evergreen since its wiry stems are bright green, providing year-round greenery and distinctive texture.

Kew broom grows at a moderate to fast rate, and is tough and durable. It is not fussy about soil type, but prefers full sun. Set plants from 1-gallon containers 3 to 4 feet apart. It is hardy to 5°F.

Duchesnia indica
Indian Strawberry, Mock Strawberry

Zones: 5-10. To 3-6 inches, spreading to 3 feet.
Deciduous or evergreen. Flowering.

Indian strawberry is one of relatively few ground covers that does well in shady, dry areas. It's useful under trees and high shrubs, and also does well in full sun. It spreads rapidly by slender surface runners, covering large expanses of ground.

Leaves are divided into threes, like strawberry leaves, but are narrower and lighter green. They grow atop 6-inch-tall stems. Flowers are yellow, 1/2 inch in diameter, and appear in spring. The "strawberries" that follow are colorful, but dry and tasteless, though birds eat them.

Space Indian strawberry plants 12 to 18 inches apart in average to rich soil. Prefers sun but will tolerate partial shade. Plants grow taller and lusher given ample water and a rich soil. It is hardy to −20°F.

Kew broom (*Cytisus x kewensis*) scrambles over rocky embankments and produces a spectacular floral display in midspring.

The three-parted leaves of Indian strawberry (*Duchesnia indica*) offer a carpet with a beautiful quilted texture to shady or sunny spots.

Fine-textured needlelike foliage and a glorious floral show in early spring make spring heath (*Erica carnea*) a prized ground cover.

Variegated forms of wintercreeper (*Euonymus fortunei radicans*) add striking color contrast to the landscape year round.

The tufted clumps of blue fescue (*Festuca ovina glauca*) have a fine texture.

Erica carnea
Spring Heath
Zones: 4-8. To 6-18 inches, spreads to 2 feet.
Evergreen. Flowering.

Spring heath is valued for its fine-textured foliage and its profusion of tiny flowers that bloom in late winter or early spring. It's a durable, mounding plant that's useful for planting in small decorative groups or massing on slopes.

Flowers are white or shades of red and pink and similar in form to flowers of heather, *Calluna vulgaris*. They are borne in dense clusters at branch tips. Needlelike foliage is gray-green and woolly textured.

There are many related species, varying widely in size, flower color, and hardiness. Some tolerate lime soil. The most popular are *E. cinerea* and *E. vagans* and their many varieties.

Spring heath prefers moist, acid soil. Grow in sun or partial shade. Space plants 1 to 2 feet apart. May be propagated from cuttings taken in August. Hardy to −10°F.

Euonymus fortunei radicans
Wintercreeper
Zones: 4-8. To 1-2 feet, spreads to 20 feet.
Evergreen.

Tough as it is beautiful, this spreading vine endures temperatures of −20°F and is also more tolerant of desert heat than English ivy, *Hedera helix*. It takes full sun or deep shade and grows in any soil. It is a versatile ground cover, useful for ornament in small or large areas, including steep banks.

Wintercreeper sprawls to 20 feet or more, and as a vine it can be used for dense coverage of tree trunks or structures. As a ground cover, it spreads rapidly, mounding slowly to about 2 feet high.

Leaves are typically shiny, dark green, oval, 1 to 2-1/2 inches long, with finely toothed edges. Brightly variegated varieties are available and make pleasing color contrasts to all-green shrubs and ground covers. Flowers are inconspicuous.

'Canadian Variegated' has small waxy leaves edged white; grows 18 inches high, spreading 3 feet wide. 'Carrierei' has green leaves and orange fruit. 'Colorata' (purple-leaf euonymus), the most popular variety, sprawls widely, has toothed green leaves turning plum color in fall. 'Dart's Blanket' is matting and wide-spreading with dark leaves and light veins. 'Gracilis' is dense, bushy, semitrailing, with variegated leaves. 'Kewensis', only 2 inches high, has fine-textured green foliage. ('Longwood' is very similar.)

Space wintercreeper plants 1 to 3 feet apart, depending on the variety, in sun or shade. An early spring mowing every year or two with a rotary mower whose blades are set high will keep plants vigorous. Euonymus scale can be a serious insect pest. Spray with dormant oil in late winter, then use diazinon or Orthene® in May and June to control. Hardy to −20°F.

Festuca ovina glauca
Blue Fescue
Zones: 5-10. To 4-10 inches, spreads to 2 feet.
Evergreen.

This ornamental grass forms rounded clumps of wiry silvery-blue leaves that create an unusual color and textural contrast to other landscape plants. Like most grasses it has graceful feathery blossoms that are held above the foliage. Planted as a ground cover, the clumps remain as individual tufts and do not spread into a carpet.

Best used in small-scale plantings as a contrast to other plants. Group as an edging for a walkway, as a ground cover beside an entryway, or as the foreground to a bed of taller ornamental grassses.

Blue fescue grows in any type of soil and does well in sun or partial shade. Space plants 6 to 12 inches apart. To keep blue fescue looking its best, you must divide clumps every second or third year. Clipping plants to the ground will also help rejuvenate their appearance. Hardy to −20°F.

Fragaria chiloensis
Wild Strawberry, Beach Strawberry

Zones: 4-8. To 6-12 inches, spreading 12-18 inches.
Evergreen. Flowering.

This glossy-leaved ground cover is one of the parents of fruiting garden strawberries. It forms an uncommonly attractive dark green mat that turns a reddish hue during winter. Flowers are an inch wide, white with yellow centers, appearing heavily in spring and intermittently in summer and fall. The 3/4-inch red berries that follow blooms are more appealing to birds than to people. Leaves, in graceful clusters of three leaflets each, are dark green.

Wild strawberry will withstand occasional light foot traffic and is useful for planting between stepping stones. Use in a woodland setting, beneath shrubs, or as an edging.

Fragaria 'Hybrid Number 25' is larger and more vigorous, and produces tasty fruit.

Space wild strawberry plants 12 to 14 inches apart in average to rich soil in sun or partial shade. Early spring mowing keeps a planting looking lush and verdant.

Galium odoratum (Asperula odorata)
Sweet Woodruff, Woodruff

Zones: 4-10. To 6-8 inches, spreading to 2 feet.
Deciduous or evergreen.
Flowering.

The flavoring for old-fashioned May wine, sweet woodruff has a long history of cultivation as a perennial herb and an ornamental in Europe and North America. It forms a pretty carpet with an appealing starlike texture created by whorls of tiny leaves. Clusters of tiny fragrant white flowers appear at stem tips in spring and early summer. Leaves have a raspy texture to the touch and a vanilla-like aroma.

Sweet woodruff has a delicate appearance that is perfect for decorating the ground under trees and

Wild strawberry (*Fragaria chiloensis*) forms a dense mat of attractive foliage that turns reddish in fall.

The unusual whorled leaves and tiny white flowers of sweet woodruff (*Galium odoratum*) make a beautiful fine-textured mat in shaded settings.

Miniature gardenia (*Gardenia jasminoides* 'Radicans') is a fragrant-flowered trailing plant that's best in small, shady areas.

A durable plant that seems most at home in woodland settings, wintergreen (*Gaultheria procumbens*) bears eye-catching edible berries in fall and winter.

African daisy (*Gazania rigens*) forms a ground-hugging carpet of evergreen foliage capped with vibrant flowers from late spring into summer.

shrubs. Use it between stepping stones in an herb garden or in a woodland garden. Will grow well in dry shaded areas as well as moist ones. It is hardy to −35°F and dies to the ground in winter in cold climates.

Sweet woodruff spreads rapidly by underground roots and can be mildly invasive. Space plants 8 to 12 inches apart. May be started from seed sown in early spring. Average to rich soil is preferred; plants need partial or full shade.

Gardenia jasminoides 'Radicans'
(*Gardenia augusta* 'Radicans')

Miniature Gardenia, Trailing Gardenia

Zones: 8-10. To 12 inches, spreading to 2-3 feet.
Evergreen. Flowering.

This low, spreading form of gardenia has all the virtues of large forms, including flowers of incomparable fragrance and beauty. Its low habit makes it perfectly suited as a ground cover for small garden spots in a warm, shaded location. Minature gardenia is an excellent companion plant for azaleas and camellias.

Flowers are an inch wide, white aging to ivory. They appear in profusion during early summer and intermittently the rest of the season. Leaves are glossy, dark green, narrow, and about 2 inches long.

Plant miniature gardenias carefully to avoid burying crowns and space 2 to 3 feet apart. Provide rich, acid soil, partial shade, and ample moisture. Hardy to 15°F.

Gaultheria procumbens

Wintergreen, Teaberry, Checkerberry

Zones: 4-8. To 6 inches, spreading to 18 inches.
Evergreen. Flowering.

This plant, native to East Coast forests, is the source for oil of wintergreen, and both its berries and its foliage have a refreshing wintergreen fragrance when crushed. Wintergreen makes a handsome and durable mat of glossy green foliage in woodland settings and is recommended only for naturalistic plantings.

Sprawling plants grow close to the ground and spread rapidly by underground runners. Dark green, leathery, oval leaves are 2 to 3 inches long. Small white bell-shaped flowers bloom in May, but are hidden by the foliage. The edible, brilliant red berries are showy in fall and winter.

Plant in moist shaded sites in rich acid soil. Space young plants about 1 foot apart. Wintergreen is hardy to −30°F.

Gazania rigens

African Daisy, Gazania

Zones: 9-10. To 6-10 inches.
Evergreen. Flowering.

Displaying a brilliant show of flowers in May or June, African daisies also bloom intermittently through the year. The dazzling flowers reach 4 to 5 inches across, either in solid colors or boldly marked, in white or a wide array of yellows, coppers, reds, oranges, or pinks.

These brilliant and varied daisies may be either clumping or trailing. Clumping varieties (*Gazania rigens*) have dense foliage up to 6 inches high and bear flowers on stems up to 10 inches tall. Leaves are toothed with silky-white hairs on the undersides, green and smooth above. Trailing varieties (*Gazania rigens leucolaena*) have untoothed, silky, grayish leaves. Yellow, sometimes orange or gold, flowers 2 to 3 inches across are held about 6 inches aboveground atop masses of long, trailing stems.

Clumping types are most useful in level or nearly level areas such as parking strips or edging. Trailing types are useful on slopes and on flat ground. Gazanias are hardy to 20°F. In colder areas they may be used as annual ground covers, because they grow and bloom rapidly.

Plant clumping varieties 1 foot apart and trailing varieties 2 to 5 feet apart in full sun in average to poor soil with good drainage. Both types like heat and are drought-tolerant. Annual mowing rejuvenates plants.

Genista lydia
Lydia Broom
Zones: 6-9. To 12 inches, spreads to
4 feet.
Deciduous. Flowering.

Lydia broom is a tough shrub with
a graceful habit. Its weeping
branches make it especially useful
on banks and for draping over
walls, where it is best displayed. In
late spring it produces a solid mass
of bright yellow, pea-like flowers at
the branch ends. Stems are lined
with narrow, bright green leaves
less than a half inch long, which
drop in fall. But it's quite attractive
with or without its leaves because
the willowy stems are green.

Lydia broom grows at a moderate to fast rate. It is hardy to
−10°F. Two other species are good
ground covers. *G. pilosa* grows 1
foot high, spreading to 7 feet. It
forms a dense mat and produces
yellow flowers. *G. sagittalis,* similar
in most respects to its cousins, has
bright green winged branchlets. It
is hardy to −20°F.

Set plants from 1-gallon cans 2
feet apart in full sun in average to
poor soil. Plants tolerate drought.

Hedera helix
English Ivy
Zones: 5-10. To 12 inches, spreads
18-24 inches.
Evergreen.

Equally at home climbing a wall or
spreading along the ground, English ivy makes one of the most
beautiful ground covers for most
climates. Leaves of the species are 3-
to 5-lobed and dark glossy green
with light green veins, remaining attractive throughout the year. Fancy-
leaved forms are available.

Extremely adaptable and vigorous, English ivy is dependable for
banks and flat areas, in both sun and
shade. A rampant grower, its deep
roots prevent erosion yet are easily
contained. Use to dress the ground
beneath trees, as an edging along
walks, or as a lawn replacement.
Used as a ground cover it grows to
about a foot high and will spread
almost indefinitely. Dwarf forms

Spectacular when flower-decked in spring and attractive year round, Lydia broom
(*Genista lydia*) is a wide-spreading plant that tolerates drought.

Forming a dense mound as wide as 7 feet
across, this broom (*Genista pilosa*) bears
masses of yellow flowers in late spring.

English ivy (*Hedera helix*) makes a
dependable evergreen cover in
both sun and shade.

Cold-hardy and widely adapted, daylily varieties (*Hemerocallis* hybrids), shown above and below, spread rapidly and flower prolifically.

Diminutive but durable, rupturewort (*Herniaria glabra*) forms a solid carpet of bright green leaves that take on a crimson cast in winter.

make excellent bulb-covers or small-area plantings.

Ivy flowers only when plants are old and have been allowed to climb, so its inconspicuous blossoms and dark blue berries are seldom seen.

There are numerous varieties of English ivy, offering variegated foliage and various leaf forms. Several of the best are: 'Hahn's Self-Branching', prefers partial shade, has small light green leaves; 'Needlepoint', a self-branching dwarf with feathery foliage; 'Fluffy Ruffles' with small leaves having wavy margins; and 'Baltica', which is especially hardy.

Algerian ivy (*H. canariensis*) is large-leaved and hardy only in Zones 8-10. Both green and white-edged forms are popular. Persian ivy (*H. colchica*) has heart-shaped leaves to 10 inches long and is hardy in Zones 6-10.

Space ivy plants 12 to 16 inches apart in rich or average soil. Tolerates full sun and deep shade; partial shade is best. In coldest areas, winter shade should be provided to prevent browning of foliage. Do not allow ivy to grow up tree trunks, because the vines can eventually strangle the trees. English ivy is hardy to around −20°F (dwarf forms are more tender).

Hemerocallis fulva and hybrids
Daylily
Zones: 2-10. To 3 feet, spreads to 18 inches.
Deciduous and evergreen.
Flowering.

When planted in masses, this favorite flower bed perennial makes an excellent ground cover to control erosion on banks and slopes. Use it in small or expansive plantings in sun or light shade in wet or dry soil.

Leaves are long, creased, and arching. They grow up from the plant's base to 2 or 3 feet tall. Flower spikes are usually 3 feet or more tall. Flowers, from 4 to 8 inches wide, last only a day, but a plant produces scores of them, day after day, often for a month or more.

Hemerocallis fulva, is an orange-flowered European native that has naturalized in the eastern states. It blooms for a long period in mid-summer and can be transplanted from the wild. Many exciting hybrids are available, varying widely in bloom time and flower color. Colors include a range of pinks, oranges, yellows, and even mahogany and purple. Double-flowered forms are also available. Blooming time may be from early to late summer, depending upon the variety. You can combine early, mid- and late-season varieties for a floral show that lasts throughout the summer months.

Some hybrids are evergreen and are hardy to −20°F. However, in cold-winter areas, they may be only partially evergreen, and benefit from mulching. Deciduous varieties are hardy between −35°F and −50°F.

Space daylily plants 12 to 18 inches apart; they will quickly spread. Any garden soil is acceptable. Though plants tolerate drought, performance is best with some water, especially during flowering. Daylilies require minimal care and are virtually trouble-free. Divide clumps in early spring.

Herniaria glabra
Rupturewort, Green Carpet
Zones: 6-10. To 3 inches, spreads to 6-8 inches.
Evergreen.

The tiny scale and apparent delicacy of this plant are misleading, for rupturewort is a durable ground cover that grows in almost any soil and tolerates occasional foot traffic. It covers small areas thoroughly and fills attractively between stepping stones.

Trailing stems spread at a moderate rate, rooting as they grow. Leaves are tiny but form a bright green, flat mass, less than 3 inches high. Leaves take on a red color during winter. Flowers are tiny and inconspicuous.

Space rupturewort plants 6 to 8 inches apart. Prefers full sun and moist soil, but tolerates partial shade. It is hardy to −5°F.

Hosta species
Hosta, Funkia, Plantain Lily

Zones: 3-9. To 6-36 inches, spreads to 18 inches.
Deciduous. Flowering.

Many species and varieties of this large genus of the lily family are admired for their beautiful foliage. Hostas are elegant planted in small groups to dress up shady spots. Combining groups of hostas with contrasting foliage color and size makes for interesting textural effects.

Hostas form clumps of leathery leaves that can be many shapes and sizes and many shades of green, including white- and gold-variegated forms. Spikes of pretty purple, lavender, or white flowers appear in late summer or early fall, but hostas are grown primarily for their foliage.

Grows best in rich, moist soil in light, partial, or full shade, though poor soil is tolerated. Space 1 to 2 feet apart, depending upon mature size. Divide crowded clumps in spring. Clip off faded flower stalks. Slugs and snails can damage foliage in some regions. Regular watering and fertilizing produce best plants. An organic mulch such as shredded bark or compost adds a clean, finished look to new plantings.

In shaded settings, the bold foliage and showy flowers of blue plantain lily (*Hosta ventricosa*), shown above, adds drama. Blunt plantain lily (*H. decorata*), below left, has brightly variegated foliage. Clumps of narrow-leafed plantain lily (*H. lancifolia*), below right, merge to create a mass of variegated foliage.

Hosta

Botanical Name/ Common Name	Zones	Flower Description	Plant Description	Comments
Hosta decorata (*H.* 'Thomas Hogg') Blunt Plantain Lily	6-9	Purple flowers in profusion from mid- to late summer.	Neat 2-ft mounds. Oval, slightly blunt leaves are 6 in. long, rich green and edged white.	Often labeled 'Thomas Hogg'.
H.d. 'Honeybells'	6-9	Lavender-lilac streaked with blue on 3-1/2-ft spikes. Fragrant.	Same as species.	Showiest flowers of any hosta; smell like gardenia.
H. lancifolia (*H. japonica*) Narrow-leafed Plantain Lily	3-9	Pale lavender blooms on 2-ft stalks in late summer.	6-in.-high clumps of slender, waxy, dark green leaves.	Variegated forms are sometimes available.
H. plantaginea (*H. subcordata*) Fragrant Plantain Lily	4-9	Fragrant white flowers on 2-ft stems, late summer or fall.	1 to 1-1/2 feet high and twice as wide with rounded bright green leaves.	
H. sieboldiana Blue-leafed Plantain Lily	3-9	White flowers in midsummer are nearly hidden by the leaves.	15 in. high and twice as wide. Bold, heavily ribbed, bluish-green leaves.	Most dramatic foliage of all hostas.
H. undulata (*H. lancifolia*) Wavy-leafed Plantain Lily	3-9	Pale lavender blooms on 18-in. stems in midsummer.	6- to 8-in.-tall leaves are green with silvery-white variegation and wavy margins. Fast-spreading.	One of the most popular hostas. Tolerates more sun than other species.
H. ventricosa Blue Plantain Lily	3-9	Lavender-purple blooms on 3-foot stalks in midsummer.	8- to 12-in.-tall dark green leaves are 5 in. wide and heavily ribbed.	Broad leaves add bold texture.

Aaron's beard (*Hypericum calycinum*) can be mass-planted to create a sweep of yellow flowers throughout summer.

Edging candytuft (*Iberis sempervirens*) forms mounds of bright evergreen foliage that are brightened with snowy flowers in late spring.

Heller's Japanese holly (*Ilex crenata* 'Helleri') creates neat mounds of fine-textured foliage in the foreground of a shrub border.

Hypericum calycinum
Aaron's Beard, Creeping St.-John's-Wort

Zones: 5-10. To 12 inches spreads to 18 inches.
Evergreen or semideciduous.
Flowering.

This ground cover seems to have the nature of cast iron, happily accepting poor soil and general neglect. It forms a beautiful dense cover of attractive evergreen foliage (semideciduous in cold areas) capped with yellow flowers through the summer. It crowds out virtually all weeds and competes successfully with tree roots for water and nutrients. There are few more serviceable ground covers than Aaron's beard for both large areas or contained areas such as parking strips. It is also an excellent cover for dry banks.

Neat medium green 4-inch leaves cover spreading stems to make a pleasingly uniform low planting. Pretty 3-inch flowers have bright yellow petals and delicate tufts of orange-yellow stamens in their centers.

Space plants 18 inches apart. Prefers full sun; tolerates partial shade. Prune plants to their bases in spring every second or third year to keep plants vigorous and dense. St.-John's-wort is hardy to −20°F.

Iberis sempervirens
Edging Candytuft, Evergreen Candytuft

Zones: 3-10. To 12 inches, spreads to 18 inches.
Evergreen. Flowering.

Usually thought of as a classic edging and rock garden plant, evergreen candytuft is also a beautiful and satisfactory ground cover for small areas. Leaves are 1-1/2 inches long, narrow, dense, dark green, and shiny. Plants form mounds about a foot high, sometimes higher. When in bloom in late spring and occasionally again in fall, plants resemble drifts of snow. Flowers are long-lasting, blooming for a full month. The rest of the year, candytuft is a rich green mat.

Use candytuft in drifts in the foreground of a shrub border, along a walkway, or in a bulb bed. Makes a showy cushion of white flowers in a rock garden or tucked in the crevices of a rock wall.

Space plants 6 to 8 inches apart. Thrives in average to rich soil in sun or partial shade. Cutting plants back after spring bloom often encourages repeat blooming in fall.

Ilex species
Holly

Zones: 6-10. To 12-36 inches, spreads to 5 feet.
Evergreen.

Some of the most handsome hollies are dwarf shrubs that make superb woody ground covers. They require little of the gardener, provide exceptional evergreen foliage, and if pollinated, many have showy berries in fall and winter, or until birds devour them.

Several species of this large genus are successful when mass-planted as a ground cover. (See chart.) Use them as a driveway border, on a slope, or in the foreground of a shrubbery border. Varieties of *I. crenata* have small leaves that resemble boxwood and are quite effective when used in large-scale plantings because the foliage is fine-textured.

Full sun is best except in areas of dry summer heat. However, hollies perform acceptably in light to medium shade, which also protects the evergreen foliage from desiccation during cold, but sunny, winter days. Rich, acid, fast-draining soil is best. Space plants a distance that is equal to two-thirds the plant's expected height (except for noted exceptions in the chart.)

Dwarf Burford holly (*Ilex cornuta* 'Burfordii Nana') is a dense evergreen shrub that grows low and spreads wide, perfect for mass-planting.

The copious quantities of bright red berries produced by dwarf Burford holly (*Ilex cornuta* 'Burfordii Nana') are showy all through fall.

Dwarf yaupon holly (*Ilex vomitoria* 'Nana') makes a dense, uniform evergreen cover suitable for mild climates and is easy to maintain.

Ilex

Botanical Name/Common Name	Zones	Size	Plant Description	Comments
***Ilex cornuta* 'Berries Jubilee'** **Berries Jubilee Chinese Holly**	6-10	To 2-3 ft tall. Spreads 3-4 ft.	Evergreen shrub with dwarf, compact, mounding habit. Leaves larger, spinier than *I.c.* 'Burfordii'. Superb display of large cardinal-red berries.	
***I. c.* 'Burfordii Nana'** **Dwarf Burford Holly**	6-10	To 1-1/2 to 5 ft tall. Spreads 6-8 ft.	Evergreen shrub with dense, globe habit. Dark green leaves with single spine at tip. Fruits heavily. Self-fruitful. Small berries are dark red.	Can be kept low by pruning. Tolerates salt spray.
***I. c.* 'Carissa'** **Carissa Chinese Holly**	6-10	To 2 ft tall. Spreads to 3 ft.	Evergreen shrub with dense spreading dwarf mounding form. Leaves smaller than *I.c.* 'Rotunda'. No fruit.	Can be kept low by pruning.
***I. c.* 'Rotunda'** **Dwarf Chinese Holly**	6-10	To 2-3 ft tall. Spreads 3-4 ft.	Evergreen shrub with low mounded form. Attractive, glossy, spiny green foliage. No fruit.	Has formal compact habit.
***I. crenata* 'Compacta'** **Compact Japanese Holly**	6-10	To 3-5 ft tall.	Evergreen shrub with dense-branching, compact habit. Glossy green foliage. Berries are black.	Tolerates city pollution.
***I. c.* 'Green Island'** **Green Island Japanese Holly**	6-10	To 2 ft tall. Spreads 4-5 ft.	Evergreen shrub with low-spreading habit. Dense branching. Small green leaves.	Grows slowly. Space plants 2 to 2-1/2 feet apart.
***I. c.* 'Helleri'** **Heller's Japanese Holly**	6-10	To 2-4 ft tall. Spreads to 2 ft.	Evergreen shrub with dwarf mounding, low-spreading form. Small dark green leaves.	Most popular dwarf Japanese holly.
***I. vomitoria* 'Nana'** **Dwarf Yaupon Holly**	7-10	To 18 in. high. Spreads to 3 ft.	Evergreen shrub. Dwarf, compact, dense. Fine gray-green foliage.	Tolerates drought once established.

Juniperus species

Juniper

Zones: 2-10. Size is variable.
Evergreen.

Low-growing, spreading species and varieties of juniper are immensely popular for ground cover plantings. There are numerous kinds to choose from, with needles ranging from bright green to blue-green and even including variegated forms. Many spread gracefully over banks, some are completely prostrate, useful to replace areas of lawn, and still others are fountain-like or mounding, effective where more height is desired.

Junipers fit well into a wide range of garden styles and will grow almost anywhere in the United States.

Most accept heat, cold, poor soil, and drought. A few are particularly adapted to coastal conditions. Best on dry, sandy, or gravelly soils.

Space plants from 6 inches to 6 feet apart, depending on the spread of the variety when it is mature. Choose a sunny well-drained spot. In hot areas, light shade is acceptable.

Juniper blight, frequently a problem in the East, is characterized by browning of branch tips. It is encouraged by overhead sprinkling. Cedar-apple rust, a gall-producing disease that infects junipers and apples, is troublesome in some areas.

There are scores of available junipers. Those top-rated for use as ground covers are listed below.

Golden pfitzer juniper (*Juniperus chinensis* 'Pfitzerana Aurea') makes a bright color contrast with green plants.

Juniperus

Botanical Name/Common Name	Zones	Size	Plant Description	Comments
Juniperus chinensis 'Fruitlandii' Fruitland Juniper	4-9	To 3 ft tall. Spreads to 6 ft.	Vigorous. Compact, dense bright green foliage.	Improved selection of *J.c.* 'Pfitzerana Compacta'.
J. c. 'Old Gold' Golden Armstrong Juniper	4-9	To 2 ft tall. Spreads to 5 ft.	Compact form with bright golden foliage.	Adds color in landscape.
J. c. 'Pfitzerana Aurea' Golden Pfitzer Juniper	4-9	To 4 ft tall. Spreads to 12 ft.	Golden-tipped foliage on spreading branches turns yellowish-green during winter.	
J. c. 'Pfitzerana Compacta' Compact Pfitzer Juniper	4-9	To 2 ft tall. Spreads to 6 ft.	Compact, dense, spreading branches. Grayish-green foliage results from white undersides of new foliage.	
J. c. 'Pfitzerana Compacta Mordigan' Mordigan Pfitzer Juniper	4-9	To 2 ft tall. Spreads to 4 ft.	Very dense, low-growing. Gray-green foliage.	Good choice for compact, low-maintenance spreader.
J. c. 'Plumosa' Plume Chinese Juniper	4-9	To 2 ft tall. Spreads to 5 ft.	Broad, spreading shrub. Horizontal branches are plume-shaped. Dark green foliage.	
J. c. 'Plumosa Aurea' Golden Plume Chinese Juniper	4-9	To 3-4 ft tall. Spreads to 3 ft.	Upright, arching branches. Bright yellow new growth. Bronzy-gold in winter.	Branches denser than 'Plumosa'.
J. c. 'San Jose' San Jose Creeping Juniper	4-9	To 1-2 ft tall. Spreads 6 ft or more.	Compact with irregular, husky branches.	Good in tub, trained as bonsai, or as ground cover.
J. c. sargentii Sargent Juniper	4-9	To 2-1/2 ft tall. Spreads 7-12 ft.	Creeping juniper. Moderately fast-growing. Holds green color in winter.	Resistant to juniper blight. Good for rock gardens, bonsai, or espalier.
J. c. sargentii 'Glauca' Blue Sargent Juniper	4-9	To 2-1/2 ft tall. Spreads 7-12 ft.	Attractive blue-green foliage.	Excellent ground cover.
J. c. sargentii 'Viridis' Green Sargent Juniper	4-9	To 2-1/2 ft tall. Spreads 7-12 ft.	Bright, light green foliage.	
J. c. 'Sea Spray' Sea Spray Juniper	4-9	To 12-15 in. high. Spreads 6-7 ft.	Dense with soft texture. Moderately fast-growing. Blue-green foliage.	Well adapted to hot and dry climates. Dense ground cover.
J. conferta Shore Juniper	6-9	To 1-2 ft tall. Spreads 8-10 ft.	Handsome weeping variety. Bluish-green foliage. Thrives in poor sandy soil and seaside conditions.	*J.c.* 'Emerald Sea' has bluer foliage; *J.c.* 'Blue Pacific' is bluer and more heat-tolerant.
J. horizontalis 'Bar Harbor' Bar Harbor Juniper	3-10	To 1 ft high. Spreads to 10 ft.	Silvery-blue foliage turns deep plum color in winter.	Fine ground cover, good on slopes, in rock gardens.
J. h. 'Blue Chip' Blue Chip Juniper	4-10	To 1 ft high. Spreads to 5 ft.	Low-mounding form. Silvery-blue foliage.	Superior ground cover. *J.h.* 'Blue Horizon' has same characteristics.
J. h. 'Emerald Spreader' Emerald Spreader Juniper	4-10	To 6-12 in. high. Spreads to 6 ft.	Very low-growing with feathery, emerald-green foliage.	Does not mound like other varieties
J. h. 'Hughes' Hughes Juniper	4-10	To 2-3 ft tall. Spreads 6-8 ft.	Graceful, low variety. Bluish-green foliage with silvery-blue new growth.	Use for color contrast.

Emerald spreader juniper (*Juniperus horizontalis* 'Emerald Spreader') grows low, does not form mounds.

Ground-hugging, wide-spreading varieties of juniper (*Juniperus* sp.) make desirable low-maintenance lawn replacements.

Blue-green varieties of juniper (*Juniperus* sp.) stand out best against a bright green lawn.

Botanical Name/Common Name	Zones	Size	Plant Description	Comments
J. h. 'Plumosa Compacta' Compact Andorra Juniper	2-10	To 1-2 ft tall. Spreads to 10 ft.	Upright, plumelike branches. Grayish-green foliage turns unique plum color in winter.	Can be espaliered.
J. h. 'Prince of Wales' Prince of Wales Juniper	3-10	To 8 in. high. Spreads 8-10 ft.	Forms dense, plush carpet. Bright green foliage has tinge of purple in winter.	Cascades over walls or ledges. Beautiful ground cover.
J. h. 'Turquoise Spreader' Turquoise Spreading Juniper	4-10	To 6-12 in. high. Spreads 6 ft.	Similar to 'Emerald Spreader' with denser foliage having bluish cast.	
J. h. 'Webberi' Webber Juniper	4-10	To 1 ft high. Spreads 6-8 ft.	Dense, compact. Center does not thin. Bluish-green foliage with purplish cast in fall.	
J. h. 'Wiltonii' Blue Rug Juniper, Wilton Carpet Juniper	4-10	To 5 in. high. Spreads to 10 ft.	Excellent dense habit. Foliage is intense silver-blue, forming an attractive carpet of blue.	One of the most popular ground cover varieties.
J. h. 'Youngstown'	2-10	To 1-2 ft tall. Spreads to 10 ft.	Very dense, upright plumelike branches, grayish-green foliage turns purplish in winter.	
J. h. 'Yukon Belle' Yukon Belle Juniper	2-10	To 6 in. high. Spreads to 10 ft.	Bright silvery-blue foliage.	Best ground cover choice in cold climates.
J. procumbens 'Nana' (*J. chinensis procumbens* 'Nana') Dwarf Japanese Garden Juniper	4-10	To 1 ft high. Spreads 4-5 ft.	Dense, low-spreader. Lush blue-green foliage.	One of the best juniper ground covers. Use in bonsai.
J. p. 'Variegata' Variegated Japanese Garden Juniper	6-10	To 2-3 ft tall. Spreads 8-10 ft.	Handsome gray-green foliage accented with patches of creamy-white.	
J. sabina 'Arcadia' Arcadia Juniper	3-9	To 18 in. high. Spreads to 4 ft.	Bright green, lacy foliage.	Resistant to juniper blight.
J. s. 'Blue Danube' Blue Danube Juniper	3-9	To 1-1/2 ft high. Spreads 5-10 ft.	Slightly erect branches with handsome blue-green foliage.	
J. s. 'Broadmoor' Broadmoor Juniper	3-9	To 1 ft high. Spreads to 4 ft.	Attractive dense, low-mounding habit. Unusual bright green foliage.	Resistant to juniper blight. Adapts well to coastal climates.
J. s. 'Buffalo' Buffalo Juniper	3-9	To 1 ft high. Spreads to 8 ft.	Lower growing than tam juniper. Feathery, soft branches with bright green foliage.	Resistant to juniper blight. Very hardy.
J. s. 'Scandia' Scandia Juniper	3-9	To 12-18 in. high. Spreads to 8 ft.	Graceful variety with wide spread. Rich, dark green foliage.	Resistant to juniper blight.
J. s. 'Tamariscifolia' Tam Juniper	3-9	To 2 ft tall. Spreads 10-20 ft.	Dense-branching. Tends to mound. Bright green foliage.	Susceptible to juniper blight. Popular as ground cover or bank cover.
J. s. 'Tamariscifolia No Blight' No-Blight Tam Juniper	3-9	To 2 ft tall. Spreads 10-20 ft.	Exceptionally hardy. Blue-green foliage.	Disease-resistant.
J. squamata 'Blue Star' Blue Star Juniper	5-9	To 2 ft. tall. Spreads 5 ft.	Slow-growing, compact. Striking silvery-blue foliage.	Good for rock gardens, bonsai, or espalier.
J. virginiana 'Silver Spreader' Silver Spreader Juniper	4-9	To 18 in. high. Spreads 6-8 ft.	Silvery-blue foliage.	Good choice for colorful ground cover.

Trailing lantana (*Lantana montevidensis*) makes an excellent colorful low border for a walkway.

Blue star creeper (*Laurentia fluviatilis*) is a delightful plant for small areas, where its petite foliage and tiny flowers are in scale with the garden.

Handsome and durable, big blue lilyturf (*Liriope muscari*) has grasslike evergreen foliage. Blue-violet flowers add interest in late summer.

Lantana montevidensis (L. sellowiana)

Trailing Lantana, Weeping Lantana

Zones: 9-10. To 36 inches, spreads to 3-6 feet.
Evergreen. Flowering.

In mild climates, trailing lantana provides a perfect bright-flowering, soil-binding bank cover and is incomparable spilling over a low wall, where it provides a mass of color. Trailing branches form dark green mounds of 1- to 3-inch-long, fine-toothed leaves. When crushed, they have a pungent aroma. Tiny flowers in clusters 1 to 2 inches across range from rosy-lilac in the species to pink, yellow, crimson, purple, and orange in varieties and hybrids. Flowers may also be bi- or tri-colored with contrasting centers.

Growing under adverse conditions that few other flowering ground covers accept, trailing lantana blooms year round in the mildest climate areas, and through warm months in moderate areas.

Space plants 2 feet apart in full sun in any garden soil. Trailing lantana is drought-resistant and seldom needs watering. Prune away dead and old, unproductive wood in spring, before new growth begins.

Laurentia fluviatilis (Isotoma fluviatilis)

Blue Star Creeper

Zones 9-10. To 3 inches, spreads to 12 inches.
Evergreen. Flowering.

This graceful small-scale ground cover is perfect for small, sunny or lightly shaded areas. It is often planted between stepping stones, where it accepts light foot traffic and atop low walls where it can spill over. Foliage is its great asset, but its intermittent sprinkling of small flowers is a good reason to choose it over flowerless covers.

Dark green leaves, usually less than 1/4 inch long, form 3-inch-high mats, higher in the shade. The light blue flowers, about 1/4 inch across, bloom through the year in mild areas but most heavily in late spring.

Space blue star creeper plants 6 to 12 inches apart. Likes rich soil and regular watering.

Liriope species

Lilyturf

Zones: 5-10. To 8-24 inches, spreads to 18 inches.
Evergreen. Flowering.

Two species of liriope are popular ground cover plants. Their distinctive low grasslike foliage makes a pleasing contrast with other plants and is attractive as an edging and small-area cover as well as making a handsome cover for fairly broad areas. Purple, blue, or white flowers bloom in late summer in compact clusters on upright spikes from 6 to 12 inches high.

Big blue lilyturf (*Liriope muscari*) is hardy in Zones 7-10. It is somewhat coarse-textured, with leaves growing to 2 feet long. Blue-violet flowers bloom in late summer, nestling among the leaves.

'Gold Band', with gold-bordered leaves; 'Lilac Beauty', low-growing, green-leaved, with deep violet flowers; and 'Majestic', 2 feet tall, with profuse deep violet flowers are excellent landscape plants. 'Silvery Sunproof', tolerant of much sun, has gold-bordered young leaves that mature to white-bordered, blooms heavily. 'Variegata', 12 to 18 inches tall, has yellow-edged leaves maturing green, and violet flowers.

Creeping lilyturf (*L. spicata*) is hardy in Zones 5-10. It has a pleasingly uniform appearance and thrives where summers are hot and winters are cold. It grows 6 to 10 inches tall with a dense fine texture. Flowers are white or pale lilac and held above the foliage.

Set big blue lilyturf plants 12 to 18 inches apart and creeping lilyturf plants 8 to 12 inches apart. Most forms look best with some shade, but full sun is acceptable in coastal areas. They hold their own around tree roots and most fairly aggressive plants, yet are unaggressive themselves.

Lonicera japonica 'Halliana'
Hall's Japanese Honeysuckle

Zones: 4-10. To 2-3 feet spreads to 3 feet.
Evergreen or semievergreen. Flowering.

This rampant vine makes a wonderful dense, binding ground cover for banks and other large expanses, but should not be planted near trees and shrubs, which it can strangle, or in a tidy garden, which it can overrun.

The blue-green leaves remain year round in warm climates, but most drop for winter in cold areas. The white flowers, famous for their fragrance, age to gold and bloom heavily in late spring and early summer and lightly during the midsummer months.

Space Hall's Japanese honeysuckle plants 2 to 3 feet apart. Prefers sun but tolerates partial shade. Thrives in poor or average soil. Severe cutting back in early spring keeps plants in check and prevents build-up of dead underbrush, which creates a fire hazard.

Mahonia repens
Creeping Mahonia

Zones: 4-10. To 2-3 feet, spreads to 3 feet.
Evergreen. Flowering.

This cold-hardy ground-covering relative of widely planted Oregon grape is particularly useful on banks to retard erosion since plants spread quickly by underground runners. It also makes an uncommonly beautiful cover for large or small beds, borders, and woodland areas.

Foliage is borne on upright stems in attractive whorls. Ten-inch compound leaves have 3, 5, or 7, 1- to 3-inch-long leaflets that are glossy, leathery, and spiny. In summer leaves are bluish-green—in fall and winter, reddish. Yellow flowers bloom in spring and blue-black berries ripen in fall.

Space creeping mahonia plants 2 to 3 feet apart in any soil type, in sun or partial shade. Drought tolerant once established.

Hall's Japanese honeysuckle (*Lonicera japonica* 'Halliana'), is a vigorous vine that covers bare ground rapidly. Its sweetly scented flowers are borne from spring into summer.

The underground runners of creeping mahonia (*Mahonia repens*) bind soil on slopes and banks. Foliage turns reddish in fall and winter.

An excellent plant for mild-climate coastal areas, prostrate myoporum (*Myoporum parvifolium*) makes a fire-retardant ground cover that tolerates salt spray.

The delicate, airy appearance of harbour dwarf heavenly bamboo (*Nandina domestica* 'Harbour Dwarf') complements other ground cover plants.

Mondo grass (*Ophiopogon* sp.) has low-growing tufts of foliage that are useful for edging walks and plantings.

Myoporum parvifolium
Prostrate Myoporum

Zones: 9-10. To 6 inches, spreads to 10 feet.
Evergreen.

Prostrate myoporum is one of the most satisfactory ground covers for coastal California, where it is an excellent cover for large areas. It is unharmed by salt spray and benefits from the cool, moist air. Fast growth, dense coverage, and strong roots make it especially useful to prevent erosion of banks, and it is fire retardant. Prostrate myoporum does well outside this narrow area only with regular watering and some afternoon shade.

This low, creeping shrub grows rapidly and is covered with neat rosemary-like leaves year round. The white flowers in summer are rather insignificant as are the purple berries in fall.

Space plants 3 to 5 feet apart. Grows in sun or partial shade, in rich or average soil with good drainage.

Nandina domestica 'Harbour Dwarf'
Harbour Dwarf Heavenly Bamboo

Zones: 6-10. To 18-24 inches, spreads to 24 inches.
Evergreen or semievergreen.

Heavenly bamboo is not a true bamboo, but a graceful shrub that resembles bamboo. Leaves are divided into many leaflets that are connected by wiry stems and arranged in attractive planes. Stems are upright and obscured by dense foliage. In full sun leaves often have a reddish cast from fall into spring, and can become brilliant red during winter. Loose sprays of small white or creamy flowers bloom at branch tips in late spring and are graceful but not showy. The bright red berries that develop on female plants are eye-catching, however.

One of several dwarf forms of the popular heavenly bamboo, 'Harbour Dwarf' spreads by underground runners at a moderate rate to make a dense, beautiful ground cover. It covers small to medium-sized areas well, and it is handsome enough to be planted where it will be seen at close range. Evergreen in most areas, it is semideciduous in extreme cold. 'Harbour Dwarf' is hardy to −10°F, though the plant freezes to the ground at −5°F and recovers in spring.

There are other low forms of heavenly bamboo, but they do not spread by underground roots to make a uniform cover. 'Compacta' is dense, to about 4 feet tall. 'Nana' (2 varieties are sold under this name) is about a foot high; one form has cupped leaflets and good color, the other is much like 'Harbour Dwarf'. 'Pygmaea', clumping and usually less than a foot high, colors brilliantly in winter.

Space dwarf heavenly bamboo plants 1 to 2 feet apart. Average to rich soil is preferred; thrives in sun or partial shade.

Ophiopogon species
Mondo Grass

Zones: 6-10. To 8-24 inches, spreads to 18 inches.
Evergreen. Flowering.

Very similar to species of *Liriope*, species of *Ophiopogon* also form tufts of grasslike foliage and spikes of purple or white flowers. Flowers are borne from early to late summer on 6- to 12-inch stems that are nestled down in the foliage, making them less showy than those of *Liriope*. Two species are top-rated and make useful evergreen ground covers in formal plantings.

White lilyturf (*Ophiopogon jaburan*) is hardy in Zones 6-10 and grows 2 feet tall. Its leaves are about 1/2 inch wide. Its variety 'Vittatus' ('Variegatus') has leaves striped with white and is frequently mislabelled *Liriope*.

Mondo Grass or dwarf lilyturf (*O. japonicus*) is the most commonly grown mondo grass. It is hardy in Zones 6-10. Leaves, 1/8 inch wide, are dark green, and light purple flowers are partly hidden by foliage. Plants make a uniform carpet 8 to 10 inches high, each clump spreading as wide.

In spring or fall, set plants 6 to 8 inches apart in full sun or shade. Best in rich, moist soil.

Osteospermum fruticosum
Trailing African Daisy, Freeway Daisy

Zones: 9-10. To 12 inches, spreads to 4 feet.

Evergreen. Flowering.

Since its introduction to gardeners by the Los Angeles County Arboretum in the late 50's and early 60's, trailing African daisy has fast become a popular ground cover for problem sites. It spreads rapidly, covering the ground with trailing stems and stalkless light green leaves, 2 to 4 inches long. Daisylike flowers, 1 to 2 inches across, are born intermittently; blanket the plants from November through March. Flowers are white with purple centers and the backsides of the petals are lavender.

African daisies make stunning mass plantings on banks and slopes and are also very pretty used in small-scale plantings above retaining walls or along walks and drives. Plants grow and cover rapidly.

Set plants 1 to 2 feet apart in full sun in rich to average soil. Though trailing African daisies are drought tolerant and survive neglect, occasional fertilizing and one or two waterings in summer will keep plants looking their best. To keep plants dense and heavy-blooming, cut back every year or two in spring before new growth begins. *Osteospermum* is hardy to 20°F.

Pachysandra terminalis
Pachysandra, Japanese Spurge

Zones: 4-9. To 6-10 inches, spreads to 12 inches.

Evergreen. Flowering.

Pachysandra, along with English ivy, periwinkle, and wintercreeper, is a ground cover star. It's both beautiful and durable, making a dense low cover for large or small areas in partial or deep shade. Plants readily spread, without being aggressive, by underground stems and compete well with tree roots.

The evergreen leaves are lustrous dark green all year round. Leaves, 2 to 4 inches long, are arranged on short upright stems in distinctive loose whorls, creating an even surface and an attractive pattern. Spikes of fragrant, rather inconspicuous fluffy white flowers appear in summer. They are usually followed by inconspicuous white berries.

This is a most satisfactory ground cover for Canada and the northern and eastern areas of the United States, although its range of adaptability is wider.

Several varieties are available. 'Green Carpet' is slightly lower and brighter green. 'Silver Edge' and 'Variegata' have white leaf margins, brighten up shady spots.

Space plants 6 to 12 inches apart. Pachysandra can be grown in sun, but the foliage turns yellowish. Partial or full shade is best and rich acid soil is preferred.

Paxistima species
Paxistima

Zones: 5-9. To 9-48 inches, spreads to 14 inches.

Evergreen.

Two species of *Paxistima*—one native to the East Coast and the other to the West Coast—make unusual ground covers for moist, shady spots. Both are tough little shrubs useful for planting beneath rhododendrons and azaleas or to use as edgings or low border plantings in small areas. They spread slowly by growing roots along their trailing branches.

Cliff-green, also called paxistima, *(P. canbyi)* grows 9 to 12 inches high; Oregon boxwood, also called myrtle paxistima, *(P. myrsinites)* can grow up to 3 feet but is easily kept at 1 to 2 feet high. Both species have narrow leaves about an inch long that are leathery, glossy, and dark green. Foliage becomes bronze-colored in winter. White or purplish flowers bloom in spring, but are quite tiny and inconspicuous.

These close relatives of rhododendrons and azaleas also like rich, acid, fast-draining soil. Will grow in sun if kept well-watered, otherwise some shade is needed. Space plants 12 to 14 inches apart.

Trailing African daisy (*Osteospermum fruticosum*) stays low to the ground, forming sweeps of colorful blossoms when mass-planted.

The foliage of pachysandra (*Pachysandra terminalis*) creates an attractive pattern that contrasts nicely with other plants.

Paxistima (*Paxistima canbyi*) has a tidy growth habit that's elegant in small-scale plantings.

Wheeler's dwarf pittosporum (*Pittosporum tobira* 'Wheeler's Dwarf') covers the ground with smooth knee-high mounds of evergreen foliage.

A tough cover for mild climates, dwarf lace plant (*Polygonum capitatum*) is frosted with pink flowers most of the year.

An attractive alternative to grass lawns, spring cinquefoil (*Potentilla tabernaemontani*) withstands light foot traffic.

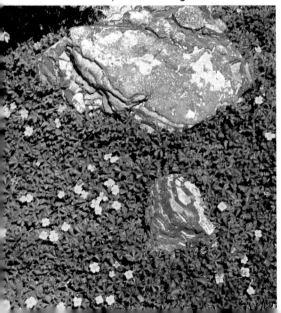

Pittosporum tobira 'Wheeler's Dwarf'

Wheeler's Dwarf Pittosporum

Zones: 8-10. To 12-24 inches, spreads to 2 feet.
Evergreen. Flowering.

This dwarf form of the popular shrub makes a neat low barrier planting when planted en masse. Each plant forms a smooth, symmetrical mound usually 1 to 2 feet high and slightly wider. The leathery leaves are rounded and slightly cupped, 2 to 5 inches long, and colored glossy dark green. The creamy-white flowers, which bloom in spring, would go unnoticed but for their strong orange-blossom scent.

Use to cover small areas, or to make a handsome evergreen foreground planting in a shrub border or along a walkway.

Space Wheeler's dwarf pittosporum plants 2 feet apart. Thrives in sun or partial shade; prefers average to rich garden soil.

Polygonum species

Knotweed, Dwarf Lace Plant, Fleece Flower

Zones: 4-10. To 6-24 inches, spreads to 2 feet.
Deciduous or Evergreen. Flowering.

This group of plants is notable for its toughness and dependability. Poor soil, drought, and heat don't phase the knotweeds; they endure adverse conditions and grow rapidly. Knotweeds are invasive, however, so use them in contained areas or where their wandering nature is a virtue. Several species are top-rated as ground covers.

Himalayan fleece flower (*P. affine*) is recommended for Zones 7-10. It grows 12 to 18 inches high and bears evergreen leaves, 2 to 5 inches long, which turn red in winter. Bright red flowers, resembling clover blossoms, appear in midsummer. Space Himalayan fleece plants 12 to 18 inches apart in any soil in sun or partial shade.

Dwarf lace plant (*P. capitatum*) grows in Zones 9-10 and is an even tougher evergreen knotweed. It grows 6 inches high and spreads to about 18 inches. Inch-long, bronze or pinkish-green leaves are rather coarse and discolor or die after a hard frost. Flowers, appearing intermittently throughout the year, and stems are pink. Even the worst soils are acceptable. Does best in sun; tolerates partial shade. Space dwarf lace plants 12 to 18 inches apart.

Compact Japanese knotweed (*P. cuspidatum compactum*) grows in Zones 4-10 and is the toughest knotweed. Mounding to around 2 feet, it spreads quickly by underground stems. Red-veined green leaves, 3 to 6 inches long, turn bright red before dropping in fall. Red flowers appear by late summer. This knotweed is excellent planted to control erosion on sunbaked slopes. It dies back to the ground in winter but reappears in spring. Space compact Japanese knotweed 1 to 2 feet apart.

Potentilla tabernaemontani (P. verna)

Spring Cinquefoil

Zones: 4-10. To 3-6 inches, spreads 12-18 inches.
Evergreen. Flowering.

This delicate-looking strawberry relative makes an attractive mat of rich green foliage sprinkled from spring to fall with yellow flowers. It provides a useful lawn alternative and accepts light foot traffic. Spring cinquefoil is very pretty used to decorate small areas seen at close range.

Each leaf is divided into 5 to 7 leaflets, each 1-1/2 inches long with toothed edges. Flowers, 3/8 inch wide, are rich yellow and resemble strawberry flowers or tiny single roses. Plants are trailing, sending out runners that root and start new plants. Growth rate is moderate.

Space plants 10 to 12 inches apart in rich, moist soil. Grows in sun or partial shade.

Pyracantha species

Firethorn, Pyracantha

Zones: 7-10. To 18-36 inches, spreads to 6 feet.
Evergreen. Flowering.

Firethorns are most often seen trained as vinelike shrubs against a wall or fence, however some varieties trail readily and make excellent ground covers. They can be used to cover large areas, including steep banks, where they control erosion. Firethorns also make effective barriers, because, as their name implies, they are thorny.

Firethorn blooms in spring, producing flat clusters of creamy-white flowers. Brilliant orange or red berries create showy clusters from fall well into winter. Foliage is lustrous and evergreen; may be semievergreen in coldest climates.

Plants tolerate any kind of soil and do well in moist or dry soil. Fireblight can be a serious disease problem in moist climates.

The following are top-rated varieties for ground cover use. 'Walderi Prostrata' grows 1-1/2 to 2 feet tall, 5 or 6 feet wide. Berries are bright red. Space plants 4 to 5 feet apart. *P. koidzumii* 'Santa Cruz' reaches 2 to 3 feet high, spreading 5 to 6 feet. Red berries are especially large. Space plants 4 to 5 feet apart. 'Leprechaun' is 24 to 30 inches tall, rounded and dense, spreading 4 to 5 feet wide. Space plants 3 to 4 feet apart. 'Tiny Tim' (Zones 7-9) reaches less than 3 feet high and as wide or wider. It is nearly thornless. Berries are cinnamon-red. Space plants 2 to 3 feet apart.

Rosmarinus officinalis
'Lockwood de Forest'
Trailing Rosemary
Zones: 7-10. To 24 inches, spreads to 4-6 feet.
Evergreen. Flowering.

This prostrate form of the old herb garden favorite isn't useful merely in the kitchen—it makes a valuable ground cover where a fine texture is desired. In areas of Mediterranean climate it is one of the toughest, handsomest, and most versatile ground covers, especially attractive on banks, spilling over walls, and along garden stairways. Rosemary is a perfect cover for a dry, sun-baked slope and scents the garden when warmed by the sun.

The sprawling shrub grows rapidly. Needle-like leaves are dark

Firethorn (*Pyracantha* sp.) is useful as an attractive barrier planting, since its vicious thorns keep people and pets away.

Trailing rosemary (*Rosmarinus officinalis* 'Lockwood de Forest') quickly covers dry, sunny sites with luxurious foliage.

A reliable favorite, sweet box (*Sarcococca hookerana humilis*) adds lush greenery to shady planting areas.

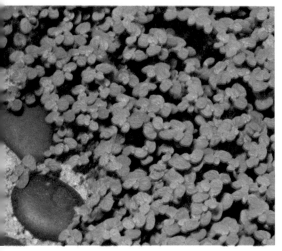

Baby's-tears (*Soleirolia soleirolii*) fills shady nooks and crannies with a thick, soft carpet of tiny-leaved foliage.

English yew (*Taxus baccata* 'Repandens'), a low spreading evergreen, grows in the light shade beneath trees.

green on top, whitish underneath, and fresh looking year round. 'Lockwood de Forest' has particularly brilliant blue, 1/2-inch flowers in winter, spring, and fall.

Space trailing rosemary plants 2 feet apart in any soil in sun or partial shade. Two or three waterings during summer, though unnecessary, make plants fuller and more lush. Tip pinching young plants encourages compactness. Occasional thinning keeps plants full.

Sagina subulata (See *Arenaria verna.*)

Sarcococca hookerana humilis
Sweet Box
Zones: 7-10. To 18-24 inches, spreads to 6-8 feet.
Evergreen. Flowering.

Sweet box can transform a barren shady spot into an inviting garden setting. This low evergreen shrub has waxy, deep green, lance-shaped leaves that are neat and attractive. Springtime flowers are hidden among leaves, but their fragrance is pleasantly noticeable. Glossy black berries appear in fall. Shrubs spread by underground stems at a moderate to slow rate.

Sweet box lends itself to forming low borders in front of larger shrubs, such as camellias and rhododendrons, and when massed, it covers large areas with lush foliage.

Space sweet box plants 30 to 36 inches apart in rich, moist soil. Does well in deep and partial shade.

Sedum species
Sedum, Stonecrop
Zones: 3-10. To 2-10 inches, spreads to 12 inches.
Evergreen succulent. Flowering.

Sedums are curious-looking succulent plants with trailing stems and rounded, juicy leaves. Clusters of colorful flowers add to their allure. Several species are top-rated. (See chart on the next page.)

Most valuable on difficult hot, dry sites, sedums also tolerate shade, though they are most vigorous in sun. They will not tolerate foot traffic, but make excellent low plants for spilling over retaining

walls, and for edging paths and patios.

Sedums prefer poor soil and scant water. Good drainage is essential. They adapt to sun or shade. In the hottest regions, some afternoon shade should be provided. All sedums grow fast, some even reproducing from their fallen leaves. Space plants as indicated in the chart.

Soleirolia soleirolii
Baby's-Tears, Angel's-Tears
Zones: 8-10. To 1-6 inches, spreads to 1 foot.
Deciduous or evergreen.

One of the finest-textured, most delicate-looking ground covers, baby's-tears forms a mossy carpet that is elegant in small garden settings. In most areas where it is adapted, it dies back in coldest weather but springs back quickly when weather warms.

Leaves are tiny, up to 1/4 inch across, and thickly cover the low stems, forming a mat 1 to 6 inches high. Flowers are inconspicuous. Plants spread at a moderate to fast rate.

Space baby's-tears plants 6 to 12 inches apart in rich, moist soil. Needs heavy to light shade; direct sun is harmful.

Taxus baccata 'Repandens'
Spreading English Yew
Zones: 6-9. To 2 feet, spreads to 10 feet.
Evergreen.

Graceful and neat year round, this dwarf, spreading shrub form of the popular yew tree adapts to banks and level areas, and can even be planted to spill over walls. Useful in well-groomed garden areas because its growth rate is slow.

Needles are glossy dark green on top, whitish underneath. Large red berries are pretty and ornament the plants in fall. However, like all parts of the plant, they are toxic if eaten.

Plant 2 to 5 feet apart in full sun or light shade in average to rich soil. Avoid spots where there is strong reflected light, because needles will

Sedum x rubrotinctum bears brilliant-hued flowers in spring and makes a fast-spreading succulent ground cover for dry, sunny areas.

Sedum lineare is one of the showiest sedums. It has light green succulent foliage year round (top photo) and is adorned with yellow flowers in spring (lower photo).

Sedum anglicum forms mounds of succulent dark green foliage capped with petite sunny flowers in spring.

Sedum

Botanical Name	Zones	Size	Plant Description	Comments
Sedum anglicum	3-10	To 2-4 in.	Small dark green, fleshy leaves. Yellow, star-shaped flowers in spring.	Ideal for covering low mounds and small banks. Space 6-10 in. apart.
S. brevifolium	3-10	To 2-3 in.	Slow-growing with small grayish-white leaves tinged with red. White, star-shaped flowers in summer.	Best used as small-scale ground cover. Must have good drainage. Space 6-10 in. apart.
S. confusum	8-10	To 6-10 in.	Light green, 1-in. leaves are clustered at branch tips. Yellow flowers in dense clusters in spring.	Not for extremely hot summer climates. Good on slopes. Space 12 in. apart.
S. dasyphyllum	8-10	To 2 in.	Small, mosslike, gray-blue leaves. Small white flowers in spring.	Good small-scale ground cover. Space 6-12 in. apart.
S. lineare (*S. sarmentosum*)	3-10	To 6-10 in.	Closely spaced, small light green leaves. Spreads vigorously. Masses of yellow flowers in spring.	One of the showiest sedums. Space 12 in. apart.
S. x rubrotinctum (*S. guatemalense*)	8-10	To 6-8 in.	Spreads vigorously. Leaves green with reddish-brown tips, 3/4 in. long, and oblong. Reddish-yellow flowers in spring.	Picks up more reddish-brown color in full sun. Space 10-12 in. apart.
S. spathulifolium	6-10	To 2-3 in.	Silvery leaves tinged red in attractive rosettes. Bright yellow flowers in late spring and early summer.	Space 6-8 in. apart.
S. spurium	3-10	To 3-4 in.	Compact mat of bronzy-green, 1-in.-long leaves. Clusters of 4-5 pink flowers held above leaves in summer.	'Dragon's Blood' has rose-red flowers. Space 6-10 in. apart.

Both the foliage and flowers of creeping thyme (*Thymus praecox arcticus*) are aromatic.

A lush and lovely creeping cover, yellow star jasmine (*Trachelospermum asiaticum*) can be kept trimmed into a neat edging.

Garden verbena (*Verbena peruviana*) carpets the ground with dense foliage that is covered with brilliant blooms during warm weather.

burn from too much heat and brightness.

Another choice form is *T. b.* 'Repandens Aurea', with golden-colored new growth.

Thymus species
Thyme
Zones: 3-10. To 2-6 inches, spreads to 10 inches.
Evergreen. Flowering.

These wonderfully fragrant, creeping herbs make excellent low ground covers, serving as lawn substitutes, fillers between stepping stones and paving stones, and covers for small-scale sunny spots. Thyme has handsome, fine-textured foliage, accepts light foot traffic, and spreads by a creeping root system. Two popular species make delightful plants for the garden.

Creeping thyme, also called mother-of-thyme (*T. praecox arcticus* or *T. serpyllum*), has 1/4-inch-long dark green leaves and forms a mat 2 to 6 inches high. During the summer months, small pink flowers in dense heads top the plant, attracting bees.

Woolly thyme (*T. pseudolanuginosus* or *T. lanuginosus*) has tiny grayish woolly leaves and forms dense mats to 3 inches high that are less uniform and more undulating than creeping thyme. During summer, it has inconspicuous white or rose flowers.

Space thyme plants 6 to 10 inches apart in sun. Tolerates partial shade. Best in average to poor soil. Clipping back tips promotes compact growth.

Trachelospermum jasminoides
Confederate Jasmine, Star Jasmine
Zones: 8-10. To 18 inches, spreads to 4-5 feet.
Evergreen. Flowering.

Clusters of nutmeg-scented, starlike white flowers and exceptionally handsome, glossy evergreen foliage make star jasmine a great favorite in mild climates. This vine happily creates a lush ground cover when its upright sprouts are clipped to encourage the stems to spread outwards. Plants spread rather quickly.

Clusters of 3/4-inch flowers bloom on short stems from spring until midsummer. Leaves are dense and lustrous, measuring 3 inches long.

Space plants 18 to 36 inches apart in rich, moist soil. In cool coastal areas plant in full sun. In hottest areas, some afternoon shade is preferred and deep shade is tolerated. Clip upright-growing stems regularly.

Yellow star jasmine (*T. asiaticum*) grows in Zones 7-10. It has smaller, darker green leaves than those of star jasmine, and smaller, yellowish flowers. Otherwise it is quite similar and has identical cultural requirements.

Verbena peruviana
Garden Verbena
Zones: 8-10. To 3-6 inches, spreads to 2 feet.
Deciduous or evergreen. Flowering.

Wherever verbena is planted, it displays a solid mass of red flowers from spring to fall. This tough and easy perennial grows so well under adverse conditions that it is a favorite ground cover in Southwest desert areas. It forms a dense, permanent cover in Zones 8 to 10, and is planted elsewhere as an annual. Use verbena as a colorful cover in both large or small areas.

Bright green leaves are small and close-set, making a dense and nearly weed-proof mat. Flowers are intense scarlet, in large, flat-topped clusters on 3- to 6-inch stems. Some nurseries offer colors other than reds: white, pink, rose, and purple.

Space plants 2 feet apart in any garden soil in full sun. Plants are drought tolerant once established.

Vinca species
Periwinkle, Myrtle
Zones: 5-10. To 6-30 inches, spreads to 1 foot.
Evergreen. Flowering.

Handsome foliage, a long season of beautiful blue flowers, plus a cast-iron constitution, make *Vinca* species all-time favorite ground covers. They dress the ground in shady spots beneath trees, spreading vigorously to cover large areas.

Myrtle *(V. minor)* is adapted to Zones 5-10. It is mildly invasive, but can be controlled by occasional pruning. The oval leaves are glossy, dark green, and 1-1/2 inches long, spaced out along trailing stems that form mats of foliage up to 6 to 12 inches deep. The flat pinwheel-shaped flowers are bright blue—periwinkle blue—and bloom most abundantly in spring but appear intermittently over the warm seasons. A white variety is sometimes available.

V. major is a larger species with leaves 2 to 3 inches long and big blue flowers that bloom abundantly in spring, more sparsely in summer. It forms upright stems 18 to 30 inches tall and spreads by underground roots. This large periwinkle is more invasive than its smaller cousin and can take over whole gardens; it is frequently seen naturalized over vast expanses of field and forest. Less cold hardy than its relative, it grows in Zones 8-10.

V. major thrives in full sun only if well watered; best in some shade. Not fussy about soil. *V. minor* should be given partial or full shade and requires good soil to look lush and healthy. Plant *V. minor* at 6-inch intervals and *V. major* at 12-inch intervals.

Waldsteinia fragarioides
Barren Strawberry
Zones: 4-9. To 2-5 inches, spreads to 6 inches.
Evergreen. Flowering.

This strawberry-less strawberry relative resembles its better-known relative, but is lower, denser, and more cold hardy. It makes an ideal ground cover for wooded, partially shaded gardens, and lends itself to large or small-scale plantings, where its foliage creates a pleasing texture.

The plants spread rapidly by surface runners that root along their length. Glossy, bright green leaves are divided into 3 leaflets, each about 2 inches long, with toothed edges. Yellow flowers, 3/4 inch across, appear in spring but do not produce berries.

Space plants 6 inches apart in sun or shade in average to rich soil. Does best with ample moisture.

Attractive evergreen foliage, bright blue flowers in spring, and a robust growth habit endear periwinkle (*Vinca minor*) to gardeners everywhere.

An ideal plant for naturalized settings, barren strawberry (*Waldsteinia fragarioides*) forms a thick carpet of pretty leaves.

Planting and Care

Ground cover plantings are generally easy to care for and do not require a great investment of money and effort to maintain them. Your greatest investments will be made during the time the planting is becoming established—thereafter maintenance is minimal. The advantages many valuable ground cover plants offer, such as drought tolerance and extreme cold hardiness, develop only after plants have become well established.

The most successful plantings are the results of careful attention paid at planting time. If your soil needs improving and you amend it generously before planting, and if you water and weed your ground covers through their first season, you will later need to give them far less attention than lawns, beds, and borders require.

WEEDS BEFORE AND AFTER PLANTING

Removing weeds and discouraging the likelihood of their recurrence before you plant the ground cover is an important first step. If you are planting where a lawn once grew, all the grass roots are best removed. It's easier to do this if you remove the turf with a spade rather than using a power tiller to churn the grass and the soil together. Cutting up the grass roots with the tiller ensures that the grass will come back to haunt you later as weeds.

If you are planting a ground cover in a previously wild or untended place, there will be many different kinds of weeds and their seeds around to cause trouble. You can till the soil and then use a soil fumigant—*best applied by professionals.* Or you can wait until warm weather has brought weeds into full foliage, then spray with a strong systemic herbicide (a weed killer

At left: A weed-eater efficiently cuts back ground covers that benefit from an annual, or semi-annual, mowing, such as Aaron's beard (*Hypericum calycinum*).

that travels throughout the plants to their roots) such as Roundup®. For the most stubborn, deep-rooted weeds, a repeat application a few weeks after the first appliction may be necessary.

Weed killers can harm weeds and ornamentals alike, so be sure to follow the directions carefully and to consult your county agricultural or extension agent or a competent nursery person, if you have any questions about how to use them. Choose weed killers that will pose no threat to the ground covers when they are planted and wait the recommended time after fumigation or herbicide application before planting.

Once ground covers are planted, weeds will continue to sprout from seeds in the soil (if soil was not fumigated) and from seed blown in or carried in by feet. Heavy mulching, hand pulling, and cultivating with a hoe will be needed to keep the weeds under control. You can save yourself trouble by killing weeds early in the season, before they have had a chance to disperse their seed.

A traditional method of weed control is spreading a 1- to 4-inch mulch of pine needles, shredded bark, wood chips, or another organic material that doesn't form a water-repellent pack or blow away in strong wind. The organic mulch discourages seed germination and makes pulling whatever weeds there are easy. The mulch also looks nice, retains moisture, insulates roots against temperature extremes, and, as it decays, improves the soil. (Remember, however, that decaying mulch can deplete the soil's nitrogen supply. One pound of ammonium sulfate per 100 square feet of ground will compensate for the loss.)

There are also chemical pre-emergents, in both granular and spray forms, such as Treflin, Surflan, Eptam, diphenamid, and Dacthal that prevent germination of

53

most seeds for specified lengths of time. Be sure to choose a pre-emergent that poses no threat to your ground cover. Read labels closely before you make a choice.

If weeds appear in spite of your efforts at prevention, you may decide to remove them by hand or hoe them as they appear. You can use a weed killer containing cacodylic acid, such as Contax Weed and Grass Killer® or Scott's Spot Grass and Weed Control®, if you use a tank sprayer with a nozzle that allows precise spot application to avoid harming the ground cover.

IMPROVING SOIL

Many soils where garden plants or lawns have been grown for a long time benefit from some soil amendment. Sandy, heavy, or infertile soils may need improvment, depending upon what kind of plants you wish to grow. Choosing ground covers, whenever possible, that are suited to your soil type can eliminate many potential problems and save you work and money. If your soil is heavy and dry, for instance, you would be wise to select a plant such as *Cistus,* which adapts readily to those conditions. With *Cistus* there would be no need to make the soil fluffy and rich, as you would need to do if you wanted to plant a ground cover such as carpet bugle.

If you are planting wide-spreading prostrate shrubs or if you are planting on a steep slope that erodes easily, you need to amend only the soil around each rootball. Other types of ground covers and planting situations usually call for amending the entire planting area.

You must evaluate several aspects of your soil—texture, pH, and fertility—to know what kind of, and how much, soil modification is desirable.

Soil texture: The types and sizes of mineral particles and the amount of organic matter that makes up a soil determine its texture. The health, even survival, of ground covers and other plants is largely determined by the texture of the soil in which they grow.

Clay soils have very tiny, microscopic particles that have a gluelike texture when wet. When moist, clay soil squeezes through your fingers in gooey ribbons; when dry, it is bricklike. Clay is a useful component of good garden soil because it holds moisture and is usually fertile, but soil that is predominantly or entirely clay allows little air to reach roots and holds water so long that roots of many plants rot.

Silty soil has slightly larger particles, but particles are still not large enough to make a good growing medium by themselves.

Sandy soils have large particles and a loose texture that allow for good aeration, in fact, roots can dry out too easily, and water and nutrients wash away too quickly. A handful of sandy soil cannot be squeezed into a ball—it crumbles instead.

Loamy soil, intermediate between clay and sandy soils, combines the best characteristics of each. It retains water and nutrients long enough to benefit plants, while still allowing aeration and fast drainage. A handful of loam squeezes into a loosely packed, crumbly ball.

Pure sand, silt, or clay soils require drastic modification before they become an ideal growing medium for most ground covers. You can modify your soil by adding copious amounts of organic matter to create an ideal loam. Composted sawdust or bark are good amendments and are available at most nurseries and garden stores. Check labels to be sure that nitrogen has been added to compensate for the nitrogen consumed by the bacteria that break down compost. Peat is a traditional soil amendment, but in most regions it is quite costly. Care must be used to wet it thoroughly as it is blended into the soil, otherwise it may form dry pockets that deflect water.

Whatever organic amendment you select to use, don't skimp on the amount. You may need up to 2 1/2 to 3 cubic yards (22 to 27 three-cubic-foot bags) per 250 square feet of soil to produce the desired result. A skimpy application is a false economy.

Soil pH: Before you complete the modification of your soil, test it or have it tested for its degree of alkalinity or acidity. You can purchase inexpensive test kits at a garden center or send soil samples to your county agricultural agent for testing. The pH of soil is measured on a chemist's scale that ranges from 0 (strongly acidic) to 14 (strongly alkaline). Midpoint, 7, is neutral. Most plants grow best in soil that is just slightly acid, around pH 6.5.

If your soil is acid, 5.5 for example, use 50 pounds of ground dolomitic limestone per 1,000 square feet. If it is alkaline, 7.5 for example, use 20 pounds of elemental sulfur per 1,000 square feet. In either case, use 1/3 more limestone or sulfur if the soil is predominantly clay and 1/3 less if it is very sandy.

Soil fertility: If you have your soil tested for pH in a laboratory, have it tested also for nutrient content so you will know the exact kind and amount of fertilizer to add. For average soil, approximately 2 pounds of an all-purpose 10-10-10 (10% nitrogen, 10% phosphorus, 10% potassium) fertilizer per 100 square feet is recommended. If you use 20-20-20 fertilizer, use half as much; if you use 5-5-5 fertilizer, use twice as much. Be careful not to apply too much nitrogen because, unlike phosphorus and potassium, it can burn plants.

After ground covers are established, particularly those that prefer rich, moist soil, they benefit from a yearly fertilizing in spring or early summer.

PLANTING

When to plant: The best planting time for ground covers depends upon your climate. If the soil freezes during winter, plant in spring as soon as the soil thaws; water regularly and provide some shade during summer. Where winters are mild, 30 to 45 days before the first frost in fall is the best planting time; the ground is still warm enough for roots to get established before winter. If summers are dry and

Soil

Clay soil has a smooth texture and retains moisture.

Sandy soil is gritty, loose, and fast-draining.

Loam soil combines the best features of clay and sandy soils.

Planting

Prepare soil by cultivating until it is loose and easy to work with, then add amendments.

Rake your prepared planting bed until the soil surface is smooth and level.

When working with plants in flats, either cut square plugs or gently pull individual plants apart.

Set plugs or individual plants in pockets made in the prepared soil, then firm soil around plants.

Space plants at an equal distance from each other, so the ground cover planting will have a uniform appearance.

Thoroughly water immediately after planting, to settle soil and eliminate air pockets around roots.

winters wet, fall planting also ensures that your ground covers will require little or no watering or sheltering from hot sunshine before they become established.

Summer planting may be unsuccessful in most climates because summer heat is too stressful to unestablished plants. In mild-summer climates ground covers may be planted successfully in summer, but special attention should be paid to watering and shading.

How to plant: Ground covers are available in flats, cell packs, 2- and 4-inch pots, and 1-gallon cans. As a rule, the price per plant increases along this scale. Many ground covers may be sold in all types and sizes of nursery containers, depending upon the maturity or size of the plant. Tiny carpeting plants such as Irish moss are usually available only in flats or cell packs. One-gallon cans are often the smallest available containers of some shrubs and vines.

Plants should be planted in moist soil that has been loosened with a hoe or spade. Remove plants gently from their containers and loosen any tightly coiled roots around their edges so roots will grow outward. If soil is being amended only in planting holes, make the holes at least twice the diameter of the nursery container and as deep. Don't expose roots to air long enough to dry them. If you are planting tiny, matting ground cover plants from flats, slice them into 2-inch-square plugs as you would brownies, using a sharp blade. Firm the soil around each newly positioned plant or plug with your hands, and water thoroughly.

Spacing: The encyclopedia entries and the planting and care chart on pages 60, 61, and 62 give recommended on-center spacing for each ground cover. (On-center means the distance from the main stem of one plant to the main stem of the next.)

The spacing for shrubby, mounding ground covers such as prostrate abelia, miniature gardenia, and many junipers is usually one-half their mature spread. Spacing at wider intervals leaves ground bare for too long, inviting growth of weeds. Spacing at closer intervals eventually results in unhealthy crowding.

Usually, small soft-stemmed trailing and rooting plants are spaced about one foot apart, sometimes closer if they are slow growers, and farther apart if fast-growers. Woody-stemmed trailers are usually spaced much farther apart, often 3 to 5 feet or more.

Spacing of all ground covers can also be influenced by the size of the plants that you use. If you find kinnikinick sold as 2- or 3-year-old plants in 1-gallon cans and also as rooted cuttings in flats, you might space cuttings as close as 6 inches and older plants as far apart as 3 feet. You might want to choose the larger plants because fewer holes would have to be dug and less soil amended. On the other hand, closely spaced cuttings would soon form a mat, and alternate cuttings could be removed when plants begin to crowd one another.

Until a ground cover planting is well established, the slope will require additional help. Plants should be planted in basins that resist erosion and hold some water. Coarse mulch and even jute netting, available at most garden supply stores, should be laid down to help ground covers get a foothold on steep banks. You might also leave annual weeds so their roots will help to hold the soil until your ground cover can do the job; cut tops of weeds down to the height of the ground cover for appearance's sake.

Watering: Until roots are well-established, just one drying out may annihilate your ground cover planting, even if the plants will be highly drought tolerant when established. It is especially important on slopes to fashion a basin around each large ground cover plant to catch rain or irrigation water for the plant's rootball.

You may hand-water or use any of the various drip or sprinkler systems that are available. Just be sure that watering is slow enough to prevent erosion and sustained enough to saturate the soil. Allow the soil to drain but not dry out between waterings. Early morning is generally the best time to water (plants dry off, so that diseases aren't encouraged). Avoid watering at midday since plants can steam to death. In cold-winter areas, thorough soaking in late autumn can prevent or lessen cold damage in winter.

SPECIAL CARE AND MAINTENANCE

Many ground covers, including English ivy, pachysandra, and hypericum, benefit from annual or semi-annual mowing. Cutting back plants to 4 to 8 inches high in early spring forces new growth and keeps the ground cover full and fresh looking. Mowing is usually accompanied by an application of nitrogen fertilizer.

Most lawn mowers cannot be adjusted high enough for mowing ground covers. Weed-eaters, gas- or electric-powered nylon line trimmers, are very effective and easy to use. Hedge shears can be used to cut back smaller plantings.

Some low-growing ground covers planted in the shade of large trees will need careful periodic raking in autumn since fallen leaves can smother plants and rob them of sunlight. In the case of taller ground covers, fallen tree leaves usually filter to the ground beneath their limbs, where they decay and contribute organic matter to the soil.

Invasive ground covers, such as hypericum and pachysandra, can become weeds if they grow into lawn areas or shrub borders where they are not wanted. The best way to keep such plants in bounds is to line the planting with header boards sunk 8 to 12 inches into the ground. Vining plants, such as English ivy, should also be clipped along their edges to keep them from moving into unwanted areas or climbing house walls.

Watering

Many types of sprinkler heads are available to use with your garden hose.

A slow stream of water from your garden hose can be used to irrigate small ground cover plantings.

Drip watering systems apply water slowly and evenly and are an efficient way to water large-scale plantings.

Mulching

Pine needle mulches hold well on slopes, help prevent erosion, and do not pack down.

Bark mulch is available in many sizes. Use uniform-sized particles to give plantings a neat appearance.

Rock mulch lasts indefinitely and does not wash away, but adds no beneficial humus to soil.

Fertilizing

Granular fertilizer promotes good growth and can be broadcast by hand. Do not allow to remain on foliage.

Liquid fertilizer sprayed on foliage produces immediate results.

Injecting fertilizer into your watering system works well when fertilizing large areas.

Cuttings taken from many ground covers will root quickly if they are simply stuck into a rooting medium that is kept moist.

It is easy to increase some types of ground covers by cutting out side shoots or rooted portions of existing plants and replanting them.

Covering trailing stems with a mound of soil stimulates roots to grow from the buried stem. Cut away rooted stems and plant.

PROPAGATION

Propagating your own ground cover plants is an inexpensive way to obtain enough plants to cover large areas. This is an especially easy undertaking with the many ground covers that self-propagate by spreading.

Cuttings: English ivy, Japanese spurge, sedum, and members of the ice plant family are among ground covers you can propagate easily by cuttings. Place short sections of stem so that at least one leaf node (area of stem where leaves were attached) is buried in flats of moist sterile sand, vermiculite, or potting soil. The rooting medium must drain fast and never be allowed to dry out. Keep the flats out of hot sun. If the climate is especially dry or windy, cover the flats with plastic or glass to maintain high humidity, but don't make the flats airtight. Commercially available rooting hormone such as Rootone® is helpful with harder-to-root plants such as juniper and gardenia.

Division: This simplest of propagating methods is successful with many ground covers. Just slice through a vigorous clump of periwinkle, for example, with a sharp-edged shovel. Remove part of the clump to start a new clump, and replace it with good soil. Plants are best divided in early spring.

Layering: Most carpeting plants creep along the surface of the ground, rooting wherever a stem rests on moist soil. You can encourage this process by covering stems with mulch, keeping the mulch moist, then cutting off and replanting the trailing stems once roots have developed.

PESTS AND DISEASES

While ground covers are generally tough, disease-and-pest-resistant plants, most of them are not entirely immune to insect pest and disease problems. When symptoms appear, quick identification and treatment can prevent extensive damage.

Diseases: Two ground covers, cotoneaster and firethorn, are susceptible to fireblight, a bacterial disease that attacks members of the rose family, causing sudden wilting and dying-back from the tips. Affected growth looks scorched. Prompt removal of every infected branch is essential; cut 6 to 8 inches below visibly affected tissue, sterilizing your pruning shears in a strong bleach solution after every cut.

Fungus diseases, including powdery mildew and root and crown rot, are encouraged by too much shade and dampness and by poor drainage. For powdery mildew, spray with benomyl or another fungicide whose label certifies it is safe for your ground cover. Junipers are sometimes attacked by juniper blight, which causes dieback; it can be controlled by a copper spray in mid- and late summer.

Pests: Snails and slugs, voracious feeders on tender leaves and stem tips, can be controlled with slug bait. If you have only a small ground cover area and prefer not to spread the poisonous bait, use a flashlight to find these nocturnal feeders and destroy them.

Spider mites, tiny spider relatives that cause plants to become sickly, pale, and sometimes yellowish or grayish, can be controlled by spraying with malathion or diazinon and a wetting agent; be sure to spray undersides of all leaves.

Various beetles can be controlled by spraying with carbaryl, diazinon, or malathion; unfortunately, beneficial ladybug beetles that feed on aphids, as well as other beneficial insects such as the praying mantis, are also killed by chemical sprays. Mealybugs and scale, which attach firmly to plant surfaces, and leaf miners, which make irregular trails beneath leaf surfaces, can be killed with Orthene® or diazinon and a wetting agent.

Various caterpillars and worms can be eradicated biologically with a spray solution of *Bacillus thuringiensis*, non-toxic to people and pets. Twig borers, which sometimes infest junipers, can be controlled by spraying with Sevin® or diazinon in early summer.

If other pests appear among your ground covers, your county agricultural or extension agent or a nursery person can help you with identification and control measures. Be sure to use all pesticides carefully and follow label directions.

Pests & Diseases

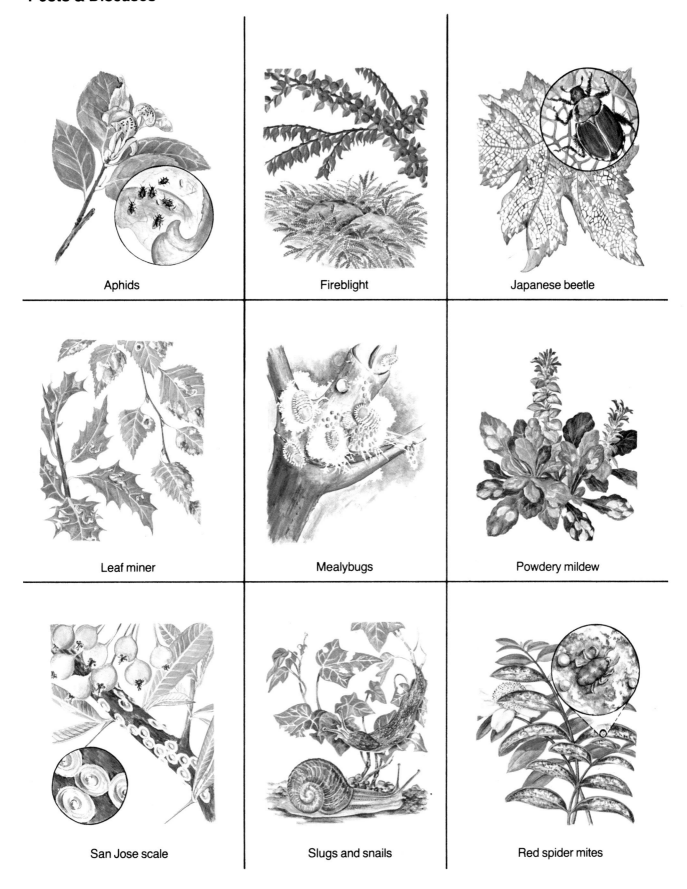

Aphids

Fireblight

Japanese beetle

Leaf miner

Mealybugs

Powdery mildew

San Jose scale

Slugs and snails

Red spider mites

Planting and Care of Ground Covers

This chart presents in simplified form basic information about the planting requirements and follow-up care for each of the ground covers discussed in this book. Use it as a quick reference to determine what conditions and care the ground covers you select will need to grow successfully. More detailed information on planting and care of particular plants is contained in the encyclopedia section.

Name	Height	Bloom Time — Showy flowers	Spring	Summer	Fall	Intermittent	Exposure — Sun	Partial Shade	Shade	Soil — Rich	Average	Poor	Water — Frequent	Average	Little	On-Center Spacing[1]
Abelia grandiflora 'Prostrata' (E and D)	To 18 to 24 in.	■		■	■		■	■		■	■		■	■	■	3-1/2 ft
Achillea tomentosa (E)	To 6 to 9 in.	■	■				■			■	■	■	■	■	■	6 to 12 in.
Aegopodium podagraria (D)	To 6 to 12 in.		■				■	■	■		■	■	■	■		2 ft
Aizoaceae (E)	To 1 to 24 in.	■	■	■	■	■	■				■[3]	■[3]		■	■	6 to 12 in.
Ajuga reptans (E)	To 2 to 4 in.	■	■					■		■			■			6 to 18 in.
Arctostaphylos uva-ursi (E)	To 5 to 10 in.		■				■			■[4]	■[4]	■[4]			■	6 in. to 3 ft
Arctotheca calendula (E)	To 6 in. to 3 ft	■	■		■	■	■			■	■	■		■	■	1 to 5 ft
Arenaria verna (E)	To 1 to 3 in.	■		■			■	■	■	■			■			To 6 in.
Baccharis pilularis (E)	To 6 to 12 in.				■		■			■	■	■		■	■	2 to 4 ft
Berberis thunbergii 'Crimson Pygmy' (D)	To 18 in.	■	■				■	■			■	■		■	■	15 in.
Bougainvillea sp. (E)	To 2 to 3 ft	■		■			■			■	■		■	■		To 3 ft
Calluna vulgaris (E)	To 6 to 24 in.	■		■	■		■				■[4]		■			1 to 2 ft
Campanula poscharskyana (D)	To 10 to 12 in.	■	■					■		■	■		■	■		1 to 2 ft
Carissa grandiflora (E)	To 18 to 24 in.	■				■	■	■		■	■		■	■		To 2 ft
Ceanothus sp. (E)	To 1-1/2 to 3 ft	■	■				■				■[3]			■	■	1-1/2 to 10 ft
Ceratostigma plumbaginoides (D)	To 10 to 12 in.	■		■	■		■	■		■	■		■	■	■	1 to 2 ft
Chamaemelum nobile (E)	To 12 in.			■			■	■		■	■		■	■	■	8 to 12 in.
Cistus sp. (E)	To 18 to 36 in.	■		■			■				■	■		■	■	1 to 4 ft
Convallaria majalis (D)	To 6 to 8 in.	■	■					■	■	■	■		■			1 to 2 ft
Convolvulus cneorum (E)	To 2 to 4 in.	■	■	■			■				■	■		■	■	To 2 ft

Name	Height	Bloom Time					Exposure			Soil			Water			On-Center Spacing[1]
		Showy flowers	Spring	Summer	Fall	Intermittent	Sun	Partial Shade	Shade	Rich	Average	Poor	Frequent	Average	Little	
Coprosma x kirkii (E)	To 2 to 3 ft					■	■	■			■	■		■	■	To 2 ft
Cotoneaster sp. (E and D)	To 6 to 36 in.	■	■				■	■		■[3]	■[3]	■[3]	■	■	■	2 to 6 ft
Cytisus x kewensis (D)	To 10 to 12 in.	■	■				■				■	■[4]		■	■	3 to 4 ft
Duchesnea indica (E and D)	To 3 to 6 in.	■	■				■	■		■	■			■		12 to 18 in.
Erica carnea (E)	To 6 to 24 ft	■	■				■	■			■[4]		■			1 to 2 ft
Euonymus fortunei radicans (E)	To 1 to 2 ft						■	■	■	■	■		■	■		1 to 3 ft
Festuca ovina glauca (E)	To 4 to 10 in.			■			■	■		■	■	■		■	■	6 to 12 in.
Fragaria chiloensis (E)	To 6 to 12 in.	■	■			■	■	■		■	■		■	■		12 to 14 in.
Galium odoratum (E and D)	To 6 to 8 in.	■	■					■	■	■	■		■	■		8 to 12 in.
Gardenia jasminoides 'Radicans' (E)	To 12 in.	■		■			■			■[4]			■			2 to 3 ft
Gaultheria procumbens (E)	To 6 in.	■	■					■	■	■[4]	■[4]		■	■		To 1 ft
Gazania sp. (E)	To 6 in. to 3 ft	■	■		■	■	■			■[3]	■[3]	■[3]		■	■	1 to 5 ft
Genista lydia (D)	To 10 to 12 in.	■	■				■				■	■[4]		■	■	2 to 4 ft
Hedera helix (E)	To 1 ft						■	■	■	■	■		■	■		12 to 16 in.
Hemerocallis hybrids (E and D)	To 3 ft	■		■			■	■		■	■	■	■	■	■	12 to 18 in.
Herniaria glabra (E)	To 3 ft						■	■		■	■		■	■		6 to 8 in.
Hosta sp. (D)	To 6 to 36 in.	■		■				■	■	■	■		■	■		1 to 2 ft
Hypericum calycinum (E and D[2])	To 1 ft	■		■		■	■	■		■	■	■	■	■	■	18 in.
Iberis sempervirens (E)	To 1 ft	■	■		■		■	■		■	■		■	■	■	6 to 8 in.
Ilex sp. (E)	To 12 to 36 in.						■	■		■[4]	■[4]		■	■		12 to 30 in.
Juniperus sp. (E)	To 6 in. to 6 ft						■				■	■		■	■	6 in. to 6 ft
Lantana montevidensis (E)	To 3 ft	■	■	■		■	■				■	■		■	■	2 ft
Laurentia fluviatilis (E)	To 3 in.	■	■	■			■	■		■			■			6 to 12 in.
Liriope sp. (E)	To 8 to 24 in.	■		■			■	■		■	■		■	■		8 to 18 in.

[1] See page 56.
[2] See encyclopedia text
[3] Fast-draining
[4] Acid

E (evergreen), D (deciduous)

Name	Height	Bloom Time					Exposure			Soil			Water			On-Center Spacing[1]
		Showy flowers	Spring	Summer	Fall	Intermittent	Sun	Partial Shade	Shade	Rich	Average	Poor	Frequent	Average	Little	
Lonicera japonica 'Halliana' (E and D[2])	To 2 to 3 ft	■	■	■			■	■			■	■		■	■	2 to 3 ft
Mahonia repens (E)	To 2 to 3 ft	■	■				■	■		■	■		■	■	■	2 to 3 ft
Myoporum parvifolium (E)	To 6 in.						■	■		■[3]	■[3]			■	■	3 to 5 ft
Nandina domestica 'Harbour Dwarf' (E and D)	To 1 to 2 ft						■	■		■	■			■	■	1 to 2 ft
Ophiopogon sp. (E)	To 8 to 24 in.	■		■			■	■		■	■		■	■		6 to 8 in.
Osteospermum fruticosum (E)	To 6 in. to 3 ft	■	■		■	■	■			■	■			■	■	1 to 2 ft
Pachysandra terminalis (E)	To 6 to 10 in.							■	■	■[4]	■[4]		■			6 to 12 in.
Paxistima sp. (E)	To 9 to 48 in.						■	■		■[4]	■[4]		■			12 to 14 in.
Pittosporum tobira 'Wheeler's Dwarf' (E)	To 1 to 2 ft		■				■	■		■	■		■	■		2 ft
Polygonum sp. (E and D)	To 6 to 24 in.	■		■			■	■			■	■	■	■	■	1 to 2 ft
Potentilla tabernaemontani (E)	To 3 to 6 in.	■	■	■	■		■	■		■			■			10 to 12 in.
Pyracantha sp. (E)	To 18 to 36 in.	■	■				■	■		■	■	■		■	■	2 to 5 ft
Rosmarinus officinalis 'Lockwood de Forest' (E)	To 2 ft	■	■		■	■	■	■		■[3]	■[3]	■[3]		■	■	2 ft
Sagina subulata. (See *Arenaria verna.*)																
Sarcococca hookerana humilis (E)	To 18 to 24 in.		■					■	■	■			■			30 to 36 in
Sedum sp. (E)	To 2 to 10 in.	■	■	■			■	■	■	■	■	■		■	■	6 to 12 in.
Soleirolia soleirolii (E and D[2])	To 1 to 6 in.					■		■	■	■	■		■			6 to 12 in.
Taxus baccata 'Repandens' (E)	To 2 ft				■		■	■		■	■			■	■	2 to 5 ft
Thymus sp. (E)	To 2 to 6 in.	■		■			■	■			■[3]	■[3]	■	■	■	6 to 10 in.
Trachelospermum jasminoides (E)	To 18 in.	■	■				■	■	■	■	■		■	■		18 to 36 in.
Verbena peruviana (E and D[2])	To 3 to 6 in.	■	■	■	■		■			■	■[3]			■	■	2 ft
Vinca sp. (E)	To 6 to 30 in.	■	■	■	■	■	■	■	■	■	■	■	■	■		6 to 12 in.
Waldsteinia fragarioides (E)	To 2 to 5 in.	■	■				■	■	■	■	■		■	■		6 in.

[1] See page 56.
[2] See encyclopedia text
[3] Fast-draining
[4] Acid

E (evergreen), D (deciduous)

Name Cross-Reference

A plant can have many common names but has only one proper botanical name. This list matches common names with their proper botanical names. The parts of a botanical name are the *genus, species,* and *variety* (or *cultivar).* The genus name signifies the general group to which the plant belongs, and together with the species name describes a particular plant. The cultivar is the name in quotes. An "x" indicates the plant is a hybrid.

Aaron's Beard .... *Hypericum calycinum*
Abelia, Prostrate .... *Abelia x grandiflora* 'Prostrata'
African Daisy .... *Gazania rigens*
African Daisy, Trailing .... *Osteospermum fruticosum*
Algerian Ivy .... *Hedera canariensis*
Angel's-Tears .... *Soleirolia soleirolii*
Baby's-Tears .... *Soleirolia soleirolii*
Barberry, Japanese .... *Berberis thunbergii* 'Crimson Pygmy'
Bellflower, Serbian .... *Campanula poscharskyana*
Bishop's Weed .... *Aegopodium podagraria*
Blue Fescue .... *Festuca ovina glauca*
Blue Star Creeper .... *Laurentia fluviatilis*
Bougainvillea .... *Bougainvillea* sp.
Box, Sweet .... *Sarcococca hookerana humilis*
Broom, Dwarf Chaparral .... *Baccharis pilularis*
Broom, Kew .... *Cytisus x kewensis*
Broom, Lydia .... *Genista lydia*
Bugleweed .... *Ajuga reptans*
California Lilac .... *Ceanothus* sp.
Candytuft, Edging or Evergreen .... *Iberis sempervirens*
Cape Weed .... *Arctotheca calendula*
Carpet Bugle .... *Ajuga reptans*
Chamomile, Roman .... *Chamaemelum nobile*
Checkerberry .... *Gaultheria procumbens*
Cinquefoil, Spring .... *Potentilla tabernaemontani*
Coprosma, Creeping .... *Coprosma x kirkii*
Cotoneaster .... *Cotoneaster* sp.
Coyote Brush, Dwarf .... *Baccharis pilularis*
Daylily .... *Hemerocallis* hybrids
Dwarf Chapparal Broom .... *Baccharis pilularis*
Dwarf Coyote Brush .... *Baccharis pilularis*
Dwarf Lace Plant .... *Polygonum capitatum*
Dwarf Plumbago .... *Ceratostigma plumbaginoides*
English Ivy .... *Hedera helix*
English Yew, Spreading .... *Taxus baccata* 'Repandens'
Fescue, Blue .... *Festuca ovina glauca*
Firethorn .... *Pyracantha* sp.
Fleece Flower .... *Polygonum* sp.
Freeway Daisy .... *Osteospermum fruticosum*
Funkia .... *Hosta* sp.
Gardenia, Trailing or Miniature ... *Gardenia jasminoides* 'Radicans'
Garden Verbena .... *Verbena peruviana*
Gazania .... *Gazania rigens*
Goutweed .... *Aegopodium podagraria*
Green Carpet .... *Herniaria glabra*
Hall's Japanese Honeysuckle .... *Lonicera japonica* 'Halliana'
Heath, Spring .... *Erica carnea*
Heather, Scotch .... *Calluna vulgaris*
Heavenly Bamboo, Harbour Dwarf .... *Nandina domestica* 'Harbour Dwarf'
Holly .... *Ilex* sp.
Holly, Chinese .... *Ilex cornuta*
Holly, Japanese .... *Ilex crenata*
Honeysuckle, Hall's Japanese .... *Lonicera japonica* 'Halliana'
Hosta .... *Hosta* sp.
Ice Plant .... *Aizoaceae*
Indian Strawberry .... *Duchesnia indica*
Irish Moss .... *Arenaria verna, Sagina subulata*
Ivy, Algerian .... *Hedera canariensis*
Ivy, English .... *Hedera helix*
Ivy, Persian .... *Hedera colchica*
Japanese Barberry .... *Berberis thunbergii* 'Crimson Pygmy'
Japanese Spurge .... *Pachysandra terminalis*

Jasmine, Confederate or Star ...... *Trachelospermum jasminoides*
Jasmine, Yellow Star .... *Trachelospermum asiaticum*
Juniper .... *Juniperus* sp.
Juniper, Chinese .... *Juniperus chinensis*
Juniper, Creeping .... *Juniperus horizontalis*
Juniper, English .... *Juniperus communis*
Juniper, Savin .... *Juniperus sabina*
Juniper, Shore .... *Juniperus conferta*
Kew Broom .... *Cytisus x kewensis*
Kinnikinick .... *Arctostaphylos uva-ursi*
Knotweed .... *Polygonum* sp.
Lace Plant, Dwarf .... *Polygonum capitatum*
Lantana, Trailing or Weeping .... *Lantana montevidensis*
Leadwort .... *Ceratostigma plumbaginoides*
Lily-of-the-Valley .... *Convallaria majalis*
Lilyturf .... *Liriope* sp., *Ophiopogon* sp.
Mahonia, Creeping .... *Mahonia repens*
Mondo Grass .... *Ophiopogon* sp.
Morning-Glory, Bush .... *Convolvulus cneorum*
Morning-Glory, Ground .... *Convolvulus mauritanicus*
Moss, Irish .... *Arenaria verna, Sagina subulata*
Moss, Scotch ..... *Arenaria verna* 'Aurea', *Sagina subulata* 'Aurea'
Moss Sandwort .... *Arenaria verna, Sagina subulata*
Myoporum, Prostrate .... *Myoporum parvifolium*
Myrtle .... *Vinca* sp.
Natal Plum .... *Carissa grandiflora*
Pachysandra .... *Pachysandra terminalis*
Paxistima .... *Paxistima* sp.
Periwinkle .... *Vinca* sp.
Persian Ivy .... *Hedera colchica*
Pittosporum, Wheeler's Dwarf .... *Pittosporum tobira* 'Wheeler's Dwarf'
Plantain Lily .... *Hosta* sp.
Pyracantha .... *Pyracantha* sp.
Red Cedar, Silver Spreader .... *Juniperus virginiana* 'Silver Spreader'
Rock Rose .... *Cistus* sp.
Roman Chamomile .... *Chamaemelum nobile*
Rosemary, Trailing .... *Rosmarinus officinalis* 'Lockwood de Forest'
Rupturewort .... *Herniaria glabra*
St.-John's-Wort, Creeping .... *Hypericum calycinum*
Sandwort, Moss .... *Arenaria verna, Sagina subulata*
Scotch Heather .... *Calluna vulgaris*
Scotch Moss .... *Arenaria verna, Sagina subulata*
Sedum .... *Sedum* sp.
Spurge, Japanese .... *Pachysandra terminalis*
Stonecrop .... *Sedum* sp.
Strawberry, Barren .... *Waldsteinia fragarioides*
Strawberry, Indian .... *Duchesnia indica*
Strawberry, Mock .... *Duchesnia indica*
Strawberry, Wild .... *Fragaria chiloensis*
Sweet Box .... *Sarcococca hookerana humilis*
Sweet Woodruff .... *Galium odoratum*
Teaberry .... *Gaultheria procumbens*
Thyme, Creeping .... *Thymus praecox arcticus*
Thyme, Woolly .... *Thymus pseudolanuginosus*
Verbena, Garden .... *Verbena peruviana*
Wild Lilac .... *Ceanothus* sp.
Wintercreeper .... *Euonymus fortunei radicans*
Wintergreen .... *Gaultheria procumbens*
Woodruff, Sweet .... *Galium odoratum*
Woolly Yarrow .... *Achillea tomentosa*
Yaupon Holly .... *Ilex vomitoria*
Yew, Spreading English .... *Taxus baccata* 'Repandens'

Index

Page numbers in bold type indicate the main entry for a plant. Page numbers in italics refer to photographs.